CRAFTING THE SOLO SHOW

A Practical Guide to Creating, Performing and Touring a One-Person Theatre Production

By Brad McEntire

© Copyright 2023 Brad McEntire. All rights reserved.

The content contained within this book may not be reproduced, duplicated or transmitted without direct permission from the author or the publisher.

Under no circumstances will blame or legal responsibility be held against the publisher or author, for any damages, reparation, or monetary loss due to the information contained within this book. Either directly or indirectly. The reader is fully responsible for his or her choices, actions and results.

Legal notice:

This book is copyright protected. This book is only for personal use. You cannot amend, distribute, sell, use, quote or paraphrase any part of the content of this book without the explicit consent of the author or publisher.

Disclaimer Notice:

Please note that the information contained within this document is for educational and entertainment purposes only. All effort has been executed to present accurate, up to date, and reliable information. No warranties of any kind are declared or implied. Readers acknowledge that the author is not engaging in the rendering of legal, financial, medical or professional advice. The content within this book has been derived from various sources, including but not limited to, the authors experience and observations.

By reading this document, the reader agrees that under no circumstances is the author responsible for any losses, direct or indirect, which are incurred as a result of the use of the information contained within this document, including, but not limited to, - errors, omissions, or inaccuracies.

Published by Dribble Funk Books

ISBN: 9798863896762

AISN: B0CKXNZDGB

Contents

PREFACE 1
   Who I am 1
   Why I'm writing this book 3
INTRODUCTION 6
   Why solo? 6
   History of Solo Performance... In A Nutshell 8
   Kinds of Solo Shows 11
CHAPTER 1 - CREATION 14
   Coming Up With Your Idea 14
   The Why? 21
   The How? 29
   Taking Notes 29
   The Frame 31
   Let it Percolate 33
   Plot and Character 36
CHAPTER 2 - GETTING IT ON THE PAGE 39
   A Word About Structure 40
   Draft 1 (Or... Learning What You Are Really Working With) .. 46
   The Rough Outline 48
   Let It Percolate... Again 50
   Skip Over Gaps 52
CHAPTER 3 – SOUNDING BOARD 54
   Get it in front of people... read it out loud... 54
CHAPTER 4 – REWRITES 57

Work in chunks 59

Opening Hook 65

Theme is purpose 66

A Word About Separating the Development Process into Distinct Drafts. 67

CHAPTER 5 – REHEARSING 69

Get it in Front of (A Few) People 69

Memorize 70

Repetition and Concentration 72

How to memorize… Or, at least, how I do it. 73

It is My Own Show. Why do I Need to Memorize? 76

Director or No Director 78

Speaking of Tech and Scenery 80

Setting a Rehearsal Schedule 82

It May Seem Lonely 86

Blocking – Don't Just Stand Around 87

Blocking for Energy 91

Keep Track of Your Progress 91

CHAPTER 6 - PERFORMING YOUR SHOW 94

Your First Show 94

Meeting Spec 96

A Word About Deadlines 97

Pay Attention 98

Remember, it is a Process 99

CHAPTER 7 – TOURING 104

Touring Kit 105

Back Up Drive 108

Observe Others 110

Factor in the Vagaries of Travel 111

Where to Stay 113

Budgeting for Touring 114

CHAPTER 8 – MARKETING PART 1 118

What do you mean "Marketing?" 119

Doing It Yourself 120

What Are You Selling? 125

Titles Are Part of the Content 126

Build Your Own Skills! 128

You Need a Platform 130

What's in a Marketing Platform? 132

   A Website 133

   The Electronic Press Kit (EPK) 138

   An Email List 149

A Word About In-Person Marketing 157

Talking About Yourself, In-Person (Especially To Press and Media People) 159

CHAPTER 9 – MARKETING PART 2 162

Postcards and Posters 162

Talk Up Your Show to Normal Folks 164

Request a Media List 167

Social Media 168

Last Word on Marketing 171
CHAPTER 10 – KEEP GOING 173
    Finding Performance opportunities 174
    Making Money as a Solo Performer 180
IN CONCLUSION 187
    Now what? 187
    Artist as instigator 189
Resources 192
    History: 192
    Writing and Structure: 192
    Memorizing and Rehearsing: 193
    DIY Media Training: 193
    Marketing: 193
    Other Resources: 194
About The Author 195

PREFACE

Who I am

I have now been performing and touring with my collection of original solo shows for over a decade and a half. I remember when I made the decision to dip my toe into the world of solo performance I looked around for a sort of guidebook to help me get started. Quite frankly, I didn't know what I was doing and the whole thing seemed very intimidating.

Writing, let alone performing, a one-person show seemed like an insurmountable task. The thought of standing on a stage, all alone, addressing a paying audience, performing an original, very personal piece of theatre filled me with apprehension.

Why did a one-person show feel so difficult? By the time I came around to solo performance, I was already pretty experienced as a theatre artist. Up to that point, in fact, I had taken quite a journey through theatre performance.

I had taken deep dives into a disparate range of subjects across the theatre arts... clowning (European and American style), puppetry, Shakespeare, the experimental works of Erik Ehn and Mac Wellman, sketch comedy, long-form improv and so on. I had taught acting, playwriting and other kinds of theatre classes to a range of ages, from elementary school kids in after-school programs to senior citizens. I had been the head of a theatre department at a public high school for several years and I had just begun teaching college theatre classes. I had collaborated with international theatre artists in Hong Kong on an original funk musical shadow puppet version of the fairy tale *Rapunzel*. I had been a produced playwright and I had served as Artistic Director for a small non-profit theatre company. Despite all that, I did not feel prepared to create, let alone, perform my own solo show.

I faced uncertainty at every turn. I questioned everything. What I wanted to know was "am I doing this right?"

I began to look around for a book that would give me no-nonsense instructions on what to expect as I created and began to perform a one-person show. I wanted a practical introduction to the format that laid out a series of guideposts and best practices for me to follow. And I could not find one.

Why I'm writing this book

Since I originally started performing and touring with my solo shows I have racked up a great deal of experience both on the creation as well as the performance and production side of things. As of this writing, I have created four solo shows for myself and an additional one to be performed by a skilled actress.

I have worked as a consultant to other solo performers, serving as a mixture of script doctor and coach. I have directed a handful of solo shows, written by others as well as by myself. I have produced my own solo performance festival. I have served as the moderator of a solo performance website. I'll put my bio at the end of this book if you want to read about my credentials, but for now, I bring all of this up because I feel I've seen solo performance from enough perspectives and performed enough of my own work that I feel I'm finally in a position to share my experiences. I believe I can supply some useful tips, techniques and outlooks on the field. So, with just a hint of residual Imposter Syndrome, I've finally decided to set stuff down on the page.

The late editor Robert Gottlieb once stated that "publishing is making public your own enthusiasm." At long last, I feel I have the enthusiasm as well as a small modicum of expertise to share.

I wanted to write the kind of book I was looking for when I began my journey in solo performance. I have set out to record some of my experiences and hard-won lessons. What I wanted was to get in the weeds a bit. I didn't just want generalizations and vague advice, I wanted to climb inside the process a bit, and invite you along.

As I went through the process of putting this book together, I realized I had a few things to say. In fact, I was surprised at just how verbose this whole thing became. I have come to discover there is, of course, no single "right way." There is simply the way that best gets across the message of what the performer is trying to say to the audience. That can change depending on the nature of the show and depending on the performer who is presenting that show. There are many ways to get that show put together and get that message across.

With all that said, I do believe there are strong choices to be made. There are also detrimental, or at least, time and energy-wasting avenues to wander down for the beginning solo performer. My hope is that I can save you a bit of time and energy. I can lay down a very rough map. It may not show the specific path, but it will give a good indication of the direction you should head.

Before we move forward, I have a general note. I will be the first to admit I certainly don't know everything about solo performance. Far from it. One of the really pleasurable things about the format is that there is so much to discover. I am continually learning. Additionally, the field is constantly changing and evolving as an art form. Solo performance is a moving target.

On top of all this, though I feel I'm somewhat above serviceable, I am by no means the world's greatest playwright or performer. There are plenty of solo performers with more experience who have created and toured more shows, to farther flung venues. I offer the only thing I can: my own experience. Lots of other performers have found lots of other ways of doing things.

    I am also just starting to sit down and write this during the latter part of 2022. The world has just pulled through a global pandemic. I bring this up because I am not quite sure what is on the horizon. Solo performance, like any other art form, continues to develop. I am sure some of what I am writing (especially mentions of technology and social media) will be dated for readers in the future.

    Lastly, the readers of this book will no doubt find advice that works for their particular situation, as well as other pieces of advice that simply do not apply. The aim of this book is to be suggestive rather than prescriptive, so feel free to cherry-pick what is useful to you and leave the rest.

    I am sincerely grateful that you are reading this and that I can be of service to you. All the best on your creative adventure ahead.

                                              ~ Brad McEntire
                                               November 2022

INTRODUCTION

Why solo?

Theatre has been on stages for a few thousand years. During the bulk of that period, plays with multiple actors have been the standard and this has been relatively uninterrupted since the days of ancient Greece. There have been rare setbacks, of course, like Puritans taking over England for a while in the 1600s or a worldwide pandemic closing theatres for a brief span of time.

I am writing this during the coronavirus pandemic of the early 2020s. It has caused most theatres in the United States to shutter their doors, much like the plague did during Shakespeare's time in Elizabethan England.

Despite these occasional setbacks traditional multi-cast plays have been doing okay for a long time. In fact, when you ask a regular person off the street what a play is, they will likely answer that a play is a bunch of people acting out a story in a theatre. So, why put together a show featuring only one actor? What is it that needs to be expressed that can't be put forward with an ensemble of performers? Are there economic, aesthetic or personal reasons? Each performer will have different reasons for creating and performing a one-person show and admittedly, some of those reasons will be more narcissistic than others.

Some folks want to showcase their ideas or their talents. Others want to have an excuse to get into the fringe festival circuit. Some may have deeply personal, heart-felt and confessional reasons. Some may want to break the fourth wall and make a deeper connection with the audience than they might otherwise. Still others want to keep the budget on the production super-low and simply create their own work.

Some performers genuinely want to translate their own personal vision of the world into a form that can be appreciated through other people's eyes and therefore add, in some small way, to everyone's richness and diversity of perception

I had a handful of reasons when I started performing one-person shows. I wanted to both write and perform original works. I particularly wanted to test myself as a performer. It is one thing to be a reliable cast member in a traditional multi-character play, but to hold the attention of an audience by yourself means one has to come face to face with the notion of whether one has actual stage presence or not. Does one have the energy required? The focus? Does one have a story worth telling and the performance chops to tell it well?

I also wanted to create something I could take full responsibility for and put together on my own timeline. Coordinating a rehearsal schedule? Rehearsals would be up to me. Design choices? Up to me. Crafting an effective marketing package? All on me. I wanted to be involved in the total creation of the work, not just in a piece of its construction.

I also had an idea that I wanted to explore. I will get into this more later, but I wanted to progress beyond being an interpretive theatre artist and take a more generative role. I didn't want to pass my idea on to someone else and open it up to interpretation, and potentially dilution, by others.

I wanted to see how far I could take the idea on my own. If I could transform an idea into a show, could I find a place to perform it? Could I market it myself? What could I discover deeper within the piece if I performed it for many different audiences over a longer span of time than a run of few weeks. Were there discoveries to be made from touring the same piece to a variety of venues in a variety of cities? Were there unforeseen opportunities for growth? All of this, and more, interested me.

Additionally, these reasons were not in direct opposition to traditional theatre performance, but simply an alternative to it. It was an alternative I wanted to try, but the question was: where to begin?

The first thing I did, once I made up my mind I was going to put together a solo show, was to do a bunch of research. I do this whenever I get interested in some new thing. I researched the history of solo performance.

History of Solo Performance... In A Nutshell

The term solo performance is amazingly broad. It encompasses autobiographical stories, comedy acts both physical and stand-up, adaptations of literature, vaudeville and circus acts, poetry recitation, musical cabaret, magic acts and dance-theatre just to scratch the surface.

Setting aside the obvious link to storytelling and myth and other oral traditions that pre-date theatre as an art form, the one-person show actually has a surprising long history. If we think of solo performance as a dramatic presentation by a single performer upon the stage delivering a sort of monologue either in character or as a narrative expressed in the first person, then the format has a pedigree that stretches back to the earliest days of theatre. Throughout the history of theatre, from Ancient Greece to the advent of television, there have been many practitioners - the list is extensive with many variations. Most would be considered "platform performers," and the usual vehicle was farce or comedy, or mimicry - imitation and impersonation - or perhaps the dramatic reading.

One might think of writers such as Edgar Allen Poe or Charles Dickens at the lectern giving voice to the characters from their books, or Mark Twain commanding a room with tales from his published stories.

In the mid-to-latter part of the 20th century, the solo performer turned in the direction of biography: Hal Holbrook as Mark Twain, Pat Carroll as Gertrude Stein, Micheál Mac Liammóir as Oscar Wilde, Emlyn Williams as Dylan Thomas, Frank Gorshin as George Burns, Simon Callow as Charles Dickens, Julie Harris as Emily Dickenson, Zoe Caldwell as Lillian Hellman, Ed Metzger as Albert Einstein. All were uncanny impersonations, carried off with remarkable degrees of substance and power.

Beginning in the 1960s, "performance art" started to appear as an alternative to both theatre and visual art. With its context of fine art many interdisciplinary artists such as Karen Finley, Holly Hughes, Laurie Anderson, Joseph Beuys and Marina Abramović expressed themselves both within and outside the walls of galleries and theatres. By the 1990s, solo performers like Lily Tomlin, Whoopi Goldberg, Tracy Ullman, Rob Becker and Eric Bogosian developed comedy monologues to create their own collection of character sketches, sometimes writing or co-writing their shows, sometimes just performing.

In fact, the last few decades of the 20th century saw a blossoming of one-person shows from the likes of John Leguizamo, Spaulding Gray, Sarah Jones, Chaz Palminteri and many more.

As I am writing this in the third decade of the 2000s, solo shows seem to be as prevalent and as powerful as ever, with performers such as Mike Daisey, TJ Dawe, Martin Dockery, Siobhan O'Loughlin, Kate Berlant, Phoebe Waller-Bridge (to name only a few) continuing the tradition.

The full history of solo performance is incredibly rich and extensive and outside the parameters of what I hope to cover in detail in this book. However, there are several good books that trace the long history of solo performance, including *Acting Solo: The Art and Craft of Solo Performance* by entertainment historian Jordan R. Young.

Kinds of Solo Shows

Despite the many kinds of one-person shows over the years, there are a few qualities that tie them all together under the collective banner: solo performance. These qualities usually include the general dismissal of the fourth wall, audience participation or involvement in some way, a somewhat idiosyncratic message and, usually, a forty five minute to hour and half running time.

I should also note: solo performance does not *need* to be written, performed, and produced by a single person, though it often is. For the scope of this book, I will be working from the assumption that the writer and performer are the same person.

Solo performance as a term is a huge umbrella, encompassing pretty much any performance by a single performer for an audience of people (this includes variety/ circus/juggling arts, fire acts, dance-theatre, improvisation and so on, up and beyond the typical monologue-style show). Sometimes, more than one person is on the stage, with a primary performer being accompanied by a musician of some kind playing live music, as is the case of cabaret or some clown acts. This arrangement might even squeak by as solo performance. For the sake of this book, I'll deal primarily with the two kinds that are practiced most often as distinct contemporary solo theatre performances.

Solo shows basically fall - and I remind you, this is a *huge* generalization - into two camps: the actor's tour de force and the dynamic lecture.

The first tradition of "one-playing-many" has included Anna Deavere Smith, Chaz Palminteri, Sarah Jones, John Leguizamo, Dawson Nichols, Tracey Ullman, Eric Bogosian, Dan Hoyle and countless other talented writer/actors. The artists who generate shows are then required to become all (or many) of the characters in the piece, even at times performing both sides of multi-sided dialogue. This kind of solo performance offers an explicit acting challenge to the performer. Sometimes the different characters in the piece interact, as embodied by the sole performer, and sometimes they are presented one after another in a sort of "character parade" of monologue vignettes.

The lecturer kind of solo show runs the gamut from Spalding Gray, Mike Daisey, David Mogolov, Martin Dockery to Mark Twain, Charles Dickens and right on up to David Sedaris, Malcolm Gladwell and Sarah Vowell. This kind of show employs a more direct address, a less actorly technique. Instead of primarily portraying other characters, the lecturer's own personality ties the evening together. The performer acts as a sort of narrator telling a story (sometimes from a previously published book by that person), usually as a character in that story.

The lecturer variety of solo performance encompasses both autobiographical and biographical shows. In an autobiographical show the performer will share something about their own life with the audience. In a biographical show the performer presents a three-dimensional portrait and the essence of (usually) a historical person.

As different as these two kinds of solo shows are – the character parade and the lecture format - they both represent variations of the much older, and highly honorable tradition of storytelling. I will discuss the key differences between straight up storytelling and solo performance later on.

I personally have tackled both kinds and find a hybrid of the two can also work extremely well. The incomparable Ruth Draper managed to create a format that blended the two approaches seamlessly by playing a single fictional character in a piece who, by the force of her characterization and the crafting of the scenes, evokes the many other "unseen" characters on stage, with tremendous detail, that she is interacting with.

Solo performance will, of course, continue to evolve. Trends come and go. Currently, at the time of this writing, there is a trend in one-person shows featuring the performer as an extreme, rather narcissistic, fictionalized version of his or herself. These performers emphasize and ironically poke fun at the conception of the one-person show as a showcase or vehicle for fame and celebrity. Perhaps this is in response of shows like Pheobe Waller-Bridge's *Fleabag* (which went on to become a television show), Natalie Palamides' *Nate: A One-Man Show* (which was picked up by Netflix) and Mike Birbiglia's *Sleep Walk With Me* (that went on to be a movie). Examples of these recent shows that mock the desperate attempt at relevance, while also ironically showcasing the skills of the performers, would be Kate Berlant's *Kate*, Liz Kingsman's *One Woman Show* and Leo Reich's *Literally Who Cares?!*

CHAPTER 1 - CREATION

Coming Up With Your Idea

I am assuming that you have an idea for a solo show already. Otherwise, how did you come to pick up this book? But if you are still casting around for an idea worthy of being made into a one-person show, here are a few tips I have observed or developed over the years that help ideas make their way into your brain from wherever ideas live when they are not in your brain.

What bothers you? What irks you about people, about institutions, about society, about the world, about yourself?

What do you celebrate? What is joyful about people, about institutions, about society, about the world, about your own life?

Oftentimes, the same things that irk us, upon careful consideration, can be the same things worth celebrating. Except mosquitoes. Mosquitoes are the worst.

What kinds of stories affect you? Solo shows are wonderful vehicles for telling stories on the stage. Fashioning a narrative is not the only mode of performance, but it certainly one of the most wide-spread uses of the format. It should also be noted, I am a huge advocate for theatre as a narrative art form, so lot of focus of the book will be concerned with how solo performers can tell a good theatrical story on the stage. All I'm saying is that you don't have to use your show to tell a story. But if you do, think about what kind of stories speak to you as a cultural consumer.

Are you drawn to a particular kind of genre? Do you like science fiction? Horror? Comedy or drama?

The underlying theme of science fiction is humanity's fear of change. This ambivalence is often represented through advancements in technology. If you have a story that deals with aversion to change, then maybe you'll want to ground your story in the science fiction genre.

Horror involves themes that also center on fear. Instead of fear of change, horror is concerned with fear of the unknown. This is often reflected as the unknown within ourselves, like madness or psychosis, or the unknown in the outer world. This latter kind of "unknown" is often shown via some supernatural element or superstition. If you have ghosts or madness or creepy, magical things happening in your story, perhaps your show fits the horror genre.

If your story involves innocent, youthful or underdog characters struggling against authority (especially parental authority) in some way, is generally humorous and has a happy ending, then maybe you have a comedy on your hands. If you have a story that is very personal and deals with social, economic, racial, gender, sexual or any other kind of "issue" then maybe you are drawn to the genre of drama. Dramas are very personal-sized and often feature main characters that suffer defeat. Dramas have rather open endings, often raising more questions than they answer. In a drama, there is usually a serious tone with humor popping up here and there to keep it from being one note.

After questioning a bunch of solo performers in casual conversation, I find most performers overwhelmingly come up with an idea one of two ways (or a combination of the two): drawing from real-life or inspired by other art forms, narrative and otherwise.

Some solo performance "coaches" will tell you to write what you know and draw from your own life. I am always amused when I hear this advice. It is very self-evident. I mean, write what you know? What else would you write about? What you don't know?

When I conduct playwriting workshops with young writers I often give the advice to write what they would want to experience as an audience member. Make the show that you, specifically, would like to see on stage.

I do think real life is a good place to pull ideas from for a solo show. I have done it myself for nearly all my shows, but there is a risk of oversimplification in offering this approach. Let me 'splain.

A lot of performers tend to pull details and situations from their own lives. Trouble rises when that is all they do. They stop with real-life, believing that simply recounting something that actually happened to them is enough. It usually is not. Just because something happened to you, in your own life, does not make it inherently theatrical.

One of the most pathetic and boredom-inducing sentences you can hear uttered by a writer/performer putting together a show is, "But this really happened to me."

Remember, you are not presenting an on stage diary. A blow-by-blow of your own experiences is not necessary or wanted.

I'm not saying don't pull from real-life, but the most interesting shows I've seen are those that expand beyond real-life, that order random events into a cohesive story and make it worthwhile to an audience, which is ultimately who the show is for (as opposed to being for you, the performer). This little step beyond simply recounting actual life is what saves a lot of "confessional" shows from being self-indulgent and masturbatory.

No audience member ever paid hard-earned money for a ticket hoping to see you engage in your own little narcissistic experiment of therapy-as-a-stage-show. I will come back to this point in a bit.

The other way I find a lot of solo performers get ideas comes from being inspired by other pieces of art around them, especially narrative art forms: movies, television, books, masterful conversations, other shows, and so on. That is to say, they collect ideas from the culture around them.

Ever been inspired by a song you heard, or something you saw in a movie? Maybe you got an idea from something you watched on a television show, a book you picked up, a painting you encountered or even something you read in an article online? This happens to me all the time.

I'm not talking about taking an idea whole-clothe from a movie or book, though this has been done (i.e. Charles Ross' *One-Man Star Wars Trilogy*). Sometimes, though, a scene in a show will make me think of something that leads to an idea. Or, for instance, I hear a lyric in a song or remember a line of poetry and that causes a domino effect in my brain that gives me an idea. Or an idea that leads to another idea and so on.

The point here is that the culture we consume can sometimes help springboard our own ideas and should not be discounted. I think part of coming up with original ideas is simply remixing bits and pieces of a bunch of disparate things we see, hear and experience and fashioning these pieces into a new and cohesive whole.

So, pay attention to what you consume beyond simply enjoying it as entertainment. Pay attention to themes, motifs, structure and so on. Pay attention to the power of images or the impact of sounds and language. If you stay open, then you may get ideas you can use. You may get ideas that will give you more ideas.

Personal Case Study:

By way of illustration, let us look at some of the disparate things that influenced me as I was putting together one of my own shows, *Chop*.

I began writing my first solo show *Chop* in mid 2007 while I was living as an expat in Hong Kong. I had a great time and met some wonderful people, but noticed this sort of background feeling from my time there. I felt this profound sense of isolation. I had lived abroad before, but the culture and ethos of Hong Kong accentuated my identity as an American. My sense of individualism ran headlong into the whole nail-that-sticks-up-gets-hammered mentality prevalent in many Asian cultures. It wasn't debilitating or serious or anything, but it was a continual awareness in the background of my everyday life.

This sense of standing outside of the society I was living in became the backbone of that first show. So, the theme came from real life.

I had also read, years ago, a short play by Dan Dietz (great playwright who became a writer and producer on HBO's show *Westworld*). I think it was called *Trash Anthem.* In it, there was this reoccurring sound of a shovel digging into dirt (there was also a pair of talking cowboy boots, too, if I recall). That shovel sound and the stage image it presented stayed with me for years, hovering in the back of my brain. I remember thinking it was really percussive and theatrical. The memory of it served as the fodder for one of the moments in *Chop*, where a man brings an axe down into a piece of wood with a very loud and very horrifying "ka-thunk." I always felt the action and sound of a man violently swinging an axe into a length of wood was a visceral and dynamic stage image.

I also filled the show with tidbits from different parts of my life. An amazing illustrator friend of mine who I had gone to college with became a character in the piece. I pulled memories from a party I had once attended, filled with an intimidating amount of accomplished creative types, to describe one of the big set pieces in *Chop*.

One of the main characters in the piece was inspired by a young lady I hung out with after a sketch comedy show many years ago. She was Eastern European and had a thick accent. She was a friend of a friend who had come to the comedy show I had performed in that night. What stuck out to me was how striking she was and how low key. She wore a tank top and had tattoos up and down both arms. Her nickname was Rosy. I only spent that one evening talking with her over several beers, but the memory stayed with me. Her name made me think of a compass rose and the character became the directional center of the piece.

In the early 2000s, I worked as an office temp in New York City. Little aspects of "cubicle culture" bubbled up in my memories and they, too, made their way into the piece.

Back in elementary school, maybe in fourth or fifth grade, I used to spend part of my lunch breaks in the school library, looking at books filled with cheesy kid jokes. Some of those bad kid jokes also got thrown into the mix.

I bring up these disparate episodes to illustrate how you can pull in unrelated influences from your life and mix them together into a frothy narrative cocktail. All these encounters, memories and observations were thrown into the blender of my brain and became little building blocks of the narrative I was putting together.

Chop ultimately turned out to be a show about a very lost and isolated man who discovers a place to belong – inside an underground amputation fetish group.

The Why?

In the introduction I listed off a bunch of reasons someone might put together a one-person show. I listed some reasons why I started putting together solo shows. I cannot stress enough the importance of really understanding why you, as an artist, are beginning your journey to create a solo show. I believe a lot of crappy art can be headed off if the artist takes the time to be clear and honest about the purpose behind any work he or she puts out into the world. *Why* is literally the reason we do what we do?

I am going to step up onto my soapbox for a second (it won't be the last time in this book). I firmly believe a solo performer should genuinely ask himself or herself a simple question at the start of the process. The performer should then periodically continue asking that question as the piece moves through its creation: What is the WHY of your solo show?

What are you really trying to do and communicate to your audience? You can create a clever, funny or dramatic show, but if there is no sense of purpose, you will leave the audience wondering "What was the point of that?"

More to the point, by confronting your own reasons for making the piece, you will keep yourself honest and maintain a sense of clarity and purpose as you create your show.

Making something just for the sake of it, without a good reason (like, a really good reason), is a waste of energy and time.... everyone's time. Even if you put together a good show technically – good acting, good production values, maybe even some moving or funny lines – without clear purpose the show can come off without significant substance. The whole endeavor can ring hollow, frivolous and perhaps even narcissistic.

I know that I may lose some readers at this point. "Art doesn't need a reason!" they shout at the page, "Art is primal. Art is instinctual. Art exists beyond petty limitations like purpose. Art is not practical. Art is about truth and beauty and the uplifting of the human spirit."

I would agree that making art does encompass an aesthetic and spiritual dimension, but I believe there should be, you know, actual reasons for one to put art out into the world. You should have something to say and a clear need to say it. That reason should be strong and you should, to some degree, be able to articulate it. The reason should also not just be for the artist, but should take the audience into consideration as well. Who does this art serve?

I believe one of the really valuable purposes of solo performance – any art, really - is to produce thinking and introspection. The process of this contemplation affects both the artist making the piece and then, on a different level, the audience that experiences the piece.

Ask yourself what cues you can offer your audience that they can take away after experiencing your production. By cues, I mean thematic, character or narrative cues that you can instill in your audience. Inspire questions in your audience. One of the jobs of theatre is to impart moral instruction. This might sound high-minded, but really it just means that the audience can see possibilities of what to do or not to do in life from what they see on stage.

So, again, what is the reason for your show?

Doing something for no discernable reason - simply for the sake of doing it - is not a valid motivation for the solo artist. Don't just add to the noise. The solo performer should look beyond mere execution. Understanding leads to reason. Reason leads to creation.

As you work on a piece there is a *philosophical duty* just as great as - if not greater than - the *practical duty* of the actual development process. *WHY* are *YOU* doing *THIS* show?

Johann Wolfgang von Goethe put three questions to any work of art to evaluate whether that work had value. These are affectionately known as Goethe's Three Questions of Criticism. The last of the three questions is "does the work have significance?" Goethe felt a completed work of art should be worthwhile.

The "why" becomes the mission statement for your show. Once it is established and understood, the "why" acts as your true compass. It also ensures you don't put a lot of time, hard work, labor and concentration into a project that will prove to be fruitless, shallow, unimportant or overly self-indulgent.

At this point, you might be thinking, "Jeez, man, you made your points. We get it." Here is why I am going on so much about the WHY of creating a solo show.
I have observed that solo performance is a format that has garnered some negative connotations. I find a lot of folks don't fully understand the scope of the format and often label it as an exercise in narcissism. The notion seem to be that It is a format for pretentious, naval-gazing, showcase-hungry artists who feel compelled to desperately explain their personal experiences to audiences.

This biased judgment is not entirely fair. However it doesn't exist in a vacuum. There have been a lot of less-than-stellar confessional shows about a person growing up insert-background or dealing with insert-trauma or overcoming insert-injury or illness. Even these sorts of confessional shows can't be painted with a broad brush. There is a lot of room for nuance. Unfortunately, this my-life-as-the-subject kind of one-person show has overshadowed a lot of other variations of solo performance in the popular zeitgeist.

"Solo Performance," with big quote marks around it, has unfortunately become a cliché in some circles. It is a format that can be easily spoofed because there are a bunch of tropes and techniques that are easy targets for mockery.

One of the reasons I think some solo performers lean heavily on their own personal experiences to the exclusion of making the narrative a satisfying theatrical show is an unexamined confusion between what constitutes storytelling and what is called solo performance. I believe this confusion is exacerbated by the popularity in recent years of storytelling podcasts and events such as The Moth. The two formats have a lot of overlap, but in aim and in execution, storytelling and solo performance are different beasts.

Although there is a long tradition of storytellers telling folktales, ghost stories and fables over the last decade or two a more personal kind of storytelling has become very popular. The emphasis is on a real-life episode from the storyteller's life. The aim is on authenticity and vulnerability. In the neo-storytelling community, such as The Moth, the storyteller is the protagonist of a story pulled from their own life. The aim is for the story to be relatable and personal above all else. It is a different thing than theatre.

I am in no way bagging on storytelling. It is a wonderful art form and I have seen some amazing storytellers. It is, however, not what this book is focusing on. There are a few key differences between the two art forms.

Storytellers do what it sounds like. They tell. They recount. They do not perform a theatrical piece. The storyteller does not play a character. They are their own character. In fact, if I am not mistaken, in storytelling circles, the theatricality that is expected in a solo show is frowned upon by storytellers. The emphasis is to be as "real" as possible. This often means the storyteller does not write the story down. No script. A certain off-the-cuff quality is encouraged. The goal is not to have a highly polished show, but a more spontaneous, conversational recounting.

Also, storytelling usually has a short run time and covers a brief period of time. A storyteller often covers a single personal event. The recounting of that story is kept to around fifteen minutes or under. This makes sense. The audience is confronted with a person dressed in their usual clothes standing at a microphone. And they just stand there. There is not enough visual dynamics, sound design or any other form of theatricality to make it interesting enough for a longer show. This is why most evenings of storytellers involve multiple performers, one after another.

If you really want to pull a real-life event from your own life and tell it unadorned, standing on a stage in front of an audience, you may consider looking into storytelling. Matthew Dicks has a wonderful book on the subject called *Storyworthy: Engage, Teach, Persuade, and Change Your Life Through the Power of Storytelling*. I highly recommend it as a resource on contemporary storytelling.

Unfortunately, the stereotype of the self-absorbed, confessional solo performer is still part of the zeitgeist.

There has even been a slew of high profile solo shows recently that have been built on satirizing these tropes in solo performance. Kate Berlant's show *Kate*, Leo Reich's *Literally Who Cares?!* and Liz Kingsman's *One Woman Show* all take aim at solo performance as an exercise for wanna-be celebrity and insufferable self-centered performers. These performers are top-notch, and I am sure they aim mostly to entertain. Of course, the irony of presenting a solo show that parodies "Solo Performance" is part of the point.

Does this sort of emphasis on the assumed tropes and stereotypes of solo performance help the field? Beats me. It does, however, cement those stereotypes instead of rising above them. Are these sorts of shows exploitative or are they, deep down, celebratory? Will the audiences know the difference?

The other reason I am including in this chapter the questioning of "why" is because I have personally seen a lot of shows where the purpose is either weak or, at the very least, not entirely clear. Okay, maybe not a LOT, but enough that I want to address it here.

I occasionally see shows where it looks like it was put together just because, well, the artist *could*. Or it was designed so he or she could look good or simply showcase themselves, a way for the artist to say "Hey, look. I'm a talented performer…" Often, the show itself doesn't have anything really significant to say.

I sometimes walk out after watching these kinds of shows and think, "That *performer* was dynamite, but what was the *show* about?"

In my humble opinion, the aim should be for the audience to remember the show more than the performer. Or to put it another way, the lasting impression should be what is said, not who is saying it.

Perhaps you are one of these artists who consider art to be its own purpose and its own reward in a very self-fulfilling, self-justifying manner. I urge you to either make some other kind of art instead of solo performance or expand your thinking about the reasons behind your own creative impulses.

Art needs to say something to someone outside the artist him or herself. That's what makes it an expression and not just a rumination. The goal is an act of theatre, not therapy. And theatre, in particular, has to keep the audience in mind. Theatre can't exist without an audience.

There is way more than enough theatre, or any other art for that matter, by this point in history. There is no room for more noise. There is no room for masturbatory or self-indulgent art.

Art is a process, so the "why" may come after the idea has established itself a little. You may even have an outline or the beginnings of a first draft before you have pieced together exactly what you are trying to make. That is okay. Just keep in mind, from early on, "why" you are making this thing that you are making.

The "why" is the test of whether your idea has legs. If it has a good reason to exist, then move heaven and earth to bring it into being. If the why is not strong, move on to the next idea. Making solo theatre is hard work. The reason I am harping on this one point so much is because I'd hate for you to put in all the time, energy and focus just to build a strawman of a show. I also harp on it because I want to do what I can in life to see that no more bad theatre makes its ways onto the stages of the world.

So, consider what you are doing. And why are you doing it. Your show needs to say something and you need to know why it needs to say that something. Let's move on to "how" exactly it is saying what it says.

The How?

After deciding the kind of story you want to tell and why you want to tell it, you can think about how you want to present it.

This is when the actual making of the piece begins and there are several things to keep in mind as you proceed. There are several different avenues to go down as well.

Some performers write out an outline, some launch right into a first draft. Some begin making mind maps, sticking post-it notes on a wall or any number of things to get started. Whichever approach speaks to you, this whole period is what I consider the note-taking phase.

Taking Notes

Taking notes just means capturing any and all of your ideas. Sometimes (often, in fact) my ideas are initially pretty crummy. I think I have a fantastic plot twist or a really catchy line of dialogue only to realize much later on that it doesn't fit, or is super lame. That's okay.

The initial ideas often give way to better ideas, then those ideas to better ones still. Sometimes having ideas about a project works the way snowballs grow larger and larger as they roll down hill. Ideas happen both cumulatively and in really fortunate cases, even exponentially.

The important thing is to get down on paper any and especially *all* thoughts about your show idea. Let an idea happen and not record it is an invitation to that specific idea to never occur again. Inspiration is fickle and doesn't linger.

These ideas will come at random times. I have had ideas hit me while in conversation, while driving, while showering, reading, cooking, just before falling asleep, while watching a movie, at the gym, while shopping, whenever.

This is why having a project log or journal is important. We will talk about project logs in more detail later on. A project log is simply a journal for keeping track of the progress you make on your show. It is an excellent place to jot down anything that crosses your mind while you are thinking about a project. A project log or journal acts as a sort of repository for all the thoughts, observations and ideas that occur to you as you start to shape your show.

The Frame

While you are compiling your thoughts through a collection of notes, one helpful thing to think about is what role the audience might play in your show.

Unlike traditional representational theatre, with multiple actors on the stage, interacting with one another while the audience simply peeps in on the goings-on from behind a "fourth wall," the solo performance almost always uses the audience as an integral *part* of the performance.

The role of the audience is not just that of a passive spectator. The audience is an active part of the piece. The audience becomes not just who the soloist acts *for* but *with*. Many times the solo performer establishes a framing device in their play for the purpose of engaging the audience in a novel fashion.

The framing device basically sets up the role that the audience will be expected to "play." The framing device also answers basic questions about the performance such as, why is this one person talking to a group of people? It is taken for granted in traditional theatre that the audience is there and they can be acknowledged or not by the actors, but 9 times out of 10, the solo performer *must* acknowledge the audience. The way this acknowledgement happens in what I call the *frame*.

The frame can take the form of an interrogation where the audience is the silent interrogator, or as a lesson a teacher is presenting to the class (the audience), or a small child talking to an invisible imaginary friend (the audience). Really, the audience can be any character or group of characters that the performer's character(s) would communicate with for a specific purpose. The framing device lets the audience know what part they are playing in the performance.

In my own solo play CHOP, for example, the audience gets hints at the beginning and then finds out more fully near the end that they are at a sort of underground meeting and they are a group of amputation fetishists that the main character has been addressing the whole time.

Remember, the audience is not there just to *witness* the story, but to *experience* it.

I should note, this framing device is not mandatory by any stretch. The long established conventions of traditional theatre can still be used. The audience can, of course, just be the audience. For example, Ruth Draper kept her characters within the world of the play and the audience, voyeuristically, looked on without Ms. Draper's explicit acknowledgment.

I have seen many shows where the performer just stands on stage, usually as his or herself or as a character that is a thinly disguised version of the performer, and just tells a story to the audience. As long as one is careful to present a theatrical solo show rather than mere storytelling there is nothing necessarily wrong with this approach. I have even created and performed such a show where I basically present an entertaining "talk" to the audience. However, I can't help mentioning that this audience-as-audience approach can waste a great opportunity unique to solo shows. Framing the audience as a partner in the performance is something that one-person shows can do that traditional plays cannot always do. I say, take advantage of that trait of the format instead of ignoring it.

Let it Percolate

So, maybe you have an idea for a solo show, or maybe you just have a vague notion that hasn't turned into a full-fledged idea yet. Pretty much every solo performer I have met who has discussed his or her process with me has had a different approach when it comes to turning ideas into concrete performances. What I want to lay out below is the several approaches that have popped up again and again with the hope that one of these approaches might help you. I will do my best to give you both the pros and cons of each approach. Since we are dealing with the creative process here, there is not one single best way and there is not a way that is going to be perfect. Use the approach that best suits you and the show you are working on.

The first way to turn an inkling of an idea into a more fully formed conception is what I call the low-concept approach. I label I'm using here is from Greg DePaul's excellent screenwriting book *Bring the Funny*. Low-concept means the story and the presentation, the characters and plot are all relatable to real-life. You see this kind of show a lot in solo performance circles. It is often a confessional show about something that really happened to the performer in their own lives that he or she has distilled into a monologue show. Low-concept shows are usually autobiographical, non-fiction pieces that lean heavy on verisimilitude rather than on theatricality.

Low-concept approaches include shows heavy on relationships and interactions between characters. Coming-of-age shows, shows dealing with overcoming hardships (overcoming an anxiety, disease or injury) or shows where social issues are the thematic center of the story (i.e. shows about bullying, gender or racial struggles, sexual orientation, social change, activism, etc.) are often low-concept. Anna Deavere Smith's documentary style solo shows such as *Fires in the Mirror, Twilight: Los Angeles, 1992* and *House Arrest* are examples of low-concept shows. These pieces were constructed using material solely gathered from interviews with real people. The artistry comes from how Smith interpreted and performed the actual verbatim words of those she interviewed.

High-concept just means that the show really leans into the theatricality of what is on stage. In longform improv this might be called Giant Roboting. These kinds of shows are fantastical and amazing, often featuring outrageous and eccentric characters, exotic and sensational locations and most importantly, stories that could not happen in real life.

If your show involves space travel, talking animals, ghosts, beasts of yore, or magical transformations you are making a high-concept show. It will, by either its content or presentation, be highly theatrical. It might involve something that could not necessarily happen in real life.

A great example of a high-concept show would be *The Last Castrato* by Chicago playwright and performer Andy Eninger. The blurb of the show reads: Taking place in the world of opera, a man born without a penis falls in love with girl who was born with her skin inside out.

Personally, I usually begin with an idea that is low-concept then allow myself the freedom and imaginative space to develop the piece into a more high-concept show. Rocket packs, time travel, chupacabras and immortal goldfish creep into an otherwise relatable world with otherwise grounded, realistic characters.

I should note here, both concepts are valuable and neither has inherent negative or positive connotations. Calling it low-concept doesn't make it lesser and calling the other high-concept doesn't make that approach better. If you are developing a real world, true-to-life idea, then the more intimate low-concept approach is for you. If your show is highly theatrical, maybe features wild shifts in time and place, with generous sprinklings of fantasy, magic, the supernatural, sci-fi or dreams then it is probably going to be on the high-concept scale.

These approaches can be combined to various degrees. There is, as in many things, a wide swath of grey area where concepts can overlap. Depending on what you are aiming to get across, a piece can begin very grounded and relatable then gradually take off to more theatrical heights. Or you can take a very theatrical premise, such as a sci-fi story about someone with a superpower, but then explore the very relatable, realistic ramifications of the piece.

The early show of mine I have been referencing, *Chop*, features a man who grows up alone and isolated. It begins rather grounded in reality, but the story gradually becomes more and more unreal as the protagonist struggles more and more with his place in the world. The story is told from the protagonist's perspective, perhaps unreliably. The piece ascends to a penultimate scene that features a *Twilight Zone*-like dream sequence. *Chop* blends together the low and high-concept models.

Once you have a grasp on what kind of show you want to put on the stage, be it low or high-concept, my recommendation is to then turn your attention towards how you will structure your tale. This will include the nuts and bolts of structure. First, let's touch on plot and character.

Plot and Character

Aristotle put plot and character at the top of his list of elements that make up theatre. For the uninitiated, plot is simply the explicit events that happen in a story and what order those events are in. Character just means the people, or human-like entities, with certain traits that the events of the story either directly happen to or that directly take action, causing specific events to happen.

It is very difficult to put together a story for the theatre that doesn't link these two concepts and have them working in tandem. Plot is made up of what characters do. If things happen, they have to happen because of someone doing something. If nothing happens, it is usually because the characters aren't doing anything. If they don't do anything, then there is no plot. No plot means no show.

Some solo performers favor plot over character, while others favor characterization over plot. When starting out on a piece, there are, in my experience, usually two paths the creator of a solo show can take.

The first path is called the inside-out method (again, I am lifting the terminology from Greg DePaul). This is when the solo show creator comes up with character first, then figures out a premise or scenario to put him or her in. Naturally, this leads to character-driven story.

Solo shows where the character comes first in the string of ideas are often less active and dynamic than plot-driven pieces. The character is the center piece of the work and what happens is of secondary concern. The inside-out method is similar to how sketch writers write comedy sketches. They have a funny, outrageous character and then find some scenario to drop that character into.

Stand-up comedians often demonstrate the inside-out method as well. Here's a "character" with particular viewpoints and opinions who just happens to be in front of an audience. The stand-up then thinks what funny things can be said by this person (often just a slightly heightened version of his or herself) to amuse the audience.

The other kind of path would be the outside-in method. Here, the story comes first, then characters are created that these things happen to. In this approach, the solo performance creator figures out what happens, then who it happens to, in that order. This leads to plot-driven pieces.

Outside-in is, for me, an easier way to create shows. This is how most screenwriters and playwrights approach their work. What the piece is about comes first, then figuring out what kind of character is involved in these goings-ons comes next. In this way, the character serves the story and not vice versa.

Both paths have merit. Like a lot of what I talk about throughout this book, these approaches can work together and criss-cross a lot. You can start with one approach and then switch emphasis. Maybe you have an event in mind and as the character responds to this event, the personality and traits come into focus more, so that you begin placing the character in different situations.

Personally, I think having a character first then trying to manufacture a bunch of things that could happen to that character is more challenging. I favor the outside-in, plot-driven approach. But you do you. Develop the idea whichever way you feel is best for your budding idea.

CHAPTER 2 - GETTING IT ON THE PAGE

Let's start with the traditional approach to show creation. That is, I am working with the assumption that you are writing down your show in a script, then crafting it through several drafts and finally developing it on its feet through a series of rehearsals. I bring this up because it is totally possible to create a solo show and not write anything down.

Martin Dockery, for instance, is an incredibly successful and prolific storyteller who has presented his electrifying, quasi-autobiographical one-person shows at fringe festivals around the world without scripting anything. (Dockery does, however, know his way around traditional scripts. He writes multi-character plays that he also performs with other actors from time to time.)

Another example of a scriptless performer is Mike Daisey. Daisey only outlines his shows. He works extemporaneously, from show to show, from a short hand-written list on a single piece of paper. It sits on the desk in front of him as a simple prompt to spur him from one section of his show to another.

It can be argued that Dockery and Daisey are primarily storytellers who happen to fall under the label of solo performers. Though they don't work with finalized written scripts, the stories they tell gradually coalesce into a finalized form after the repetition of multiple performances.

For the purposes of this book, I am also working under the assumption that you are creating a piece with spoken words. This is also not always the case.

The great Avner the Eccentric performed his self-titled one-man show and his hilarious *Exceptions to Gravity* clown show moving from set piece to set piece without muttering a word. Performer David Gaines presented his own full-length stage adaptation of Kurasawa's film *Seven Samurai* completely in mime, offering the occasional sound effect but no dialogue. So, of course, a solo show can be created without a script and even without dialogue.

I come from a playwriting background. I write stuff down. That's just my own approach, so that's what I feel comfortable covering here. Let's start with plot structure.

A Word About Structure

You have to bring the audience along with you. That means there has to be some place to start and then someplace to go in the piece you are creating. This means there is at least some kind of structure.

Structure is just a fancy way of emphasizing that there is an order of events: a beginning, middle and end... even if you don't put them in that particular order.

Many plays have been written based on a three or five act structure. In 350 BCE, ancient Greek philosopher Aristotle, in his collection of lecture notes on the theatre, *The Poetics*, cited three parts of a play (he was specifically referring to tragedy, but in broad terms it applies pretty much across the board). These three parts are *protasis, which* is the introduction; the middle or *epitasis* which contains the crisis point and the *catastrophe,* which has the resolution to the conflict.

In the 1860s, Gustav Freytag, a German novelist and critic, observed the similarity of plots in many stories so he created a sort of pictorial graph to visually illustrate dramatic structure. Called Freytag's Triangle (you'll also see it called Freytag's Pyramid), he constructed a five-part pattern in the form of an ascending and descending spike to analyze the plot structure of dramas. We often use the terminology Freytag came up with nowadays when we talk about dramatic structure.

Freytag's Pyramid is a modification of Aristotle's structure where he transformed the basic three parts into five by adding two other levels. At the beginning he put a level he referred to as exposition. Exposition is followed by rising action, climax, falling action and then the resolution.

If you have a passing knowledge of the theatre (or any other narrative art such as novels, movies, television shows, etc.) then you are probably familiar with this sort of plot structure. However, it is always nice to have a refresher. Let's take a closer look at the five parts of dramatic structure Freytag outlined:

1. Exposition or Introduction
The exposition/introduction presents the setting (time and place), main characters (protagonist – hero/heroine, antagonist – villain), and establishes the mood or atmosphere of the world of the story before the plot kicks into gear. This is the way the world is before things start happening. It is often called the *status quo* (Latin for "the existing state of affairs").

This first part enables the reader to know more about the circumstances and the relationship of the characters with each other. We are often told of events that happened before the play started that are relevant to the story (think the death of Hamlet's dad. It happens before the play, but is hugely important to the plot). These events that affect the story that happened prior are called exposition. This is usually sprinkled in as information through the beginning of the play. Sometimes, there is a scene or a monologue that serves up a bunch of exposition called a prologue. The introduction ends when an exciting event happens leading to the conflict which impels the story to move forward.

2. Rising action

Rising action is the second part where the basic conflict has been presented and the audience is beginning to feel the rising tension associated with this conflict. At this point, the basic conflict is further complicated by the introduction of obstacles frustrating the protagonist and other characters from easily reaching their objectives. The bulk of conflict happens during the rising action. Friends become enemies and enemies become allies. Challenges are met.

3. Climax

The climax is the big turning point and this third part effects a change either for the better or for the worse in the protagonist's situation. In a comedy, the protagonist positively faces his or her obstacles and there is a great chance that things will turn out well; but in a tragedy, the conflict of the protagonist has been worsening until it ultimately turns disastrous. It should be noted, unlike in contemporary movies (usually with three act structures), the climax in Freytag's five-act arc takes place over an entire act, not a quick scene/ confrontation.

4. Falling action

The protagonist has either won or lost to the antagonist by this point. There are usually a brief series of unexpected incidents which make the final outcome a bit more suspenseful. The falling action designates that the story is heading towards its conclusion. The protagonist is returning back to a new status quo.

5. Conclusion

The conclusion is the end of the story which is sometimes called *dénouement* (not a term originally used by Freytag). This is the resolution. After conflicts are resolved, the characters resume their new normal lives. Dénouement is a French word which means untangling. The conclusion is explained and there is a metaphorical untying, or smoothing out, of the plot complexities.

There is no rule that says you have to follow a traditional three or five act structure when you are putting together your show. And even if you do, you can play around with parts of the structure.

Sometimes, especially in contemporary works, the ending comes very abruptly or there is purposely an open-ended conclusion that does not bring the story to a terminal finale.

Besides Freytag's Triangle and Aristotle's three-part structure, there are numerous other ways to plot your story. You can use Joseph Campbell's Hero's

Journey or television writer Dan Harmon's modified version of it called the Story Circle. You can use a Fichtean Curve, Kenn Adams' Story Spine or Blake Snyder's Save the Cat Beat Sheet. Heck, you could structure your solo show like the different courses of a good meal or a mix tape or the seasons.

I have seen a handful of plays structured as a series of unrelated episodes that are loosely tied together thematically. I have seen a sort of Gestalt structure with seemingly disparate scenes that build on top of each other to leave the audience with a sort of over-all cumulative impression by the end.

I have even seen a piece structured like a metaphorical Russian nesting doll where the protagonist in the story encountered a hydra of new problems every time he overcame the next step in the tale. He was comically pushed further and further from accomplishing his original goal until he just gave up and stopped.

I remember another show where the plot wound around on itself cyclically like a snake eating its own tail and by the conclusion the main character ended up right back where she had started.

Though you are free to structure the order of events in your piece however you like, audiences nowadays are pretty sophisticated. With the complex television shows, a variety of movies and constant stimulus of the internet today's theatre audiences are often rather savvy when it comes to understanding story, especially on a conceptual level.

Audiences can sense if you are skipping over important sections, or will rightfully be angered if you indicate that the story is leading up to a satisfying ending and you don't deliver. Audiences have been conditioned to listen and pick up on hints, symbols, tone and so on. They tend to notice when there are plot holes.

More important than a traditional structure is a sense of completeness in your show. You don't have to structure your show like any of the suggestions above. Really, any structure is okay, as long as it fits what you are trying to say and adds a sense of cohesion and coherence.

The only really solid way to screw up is not to have any structure at all. Random, arbitrary scenes that don't go anywhere make for a pretty unsatisfactory theatre experience.

So, here's the take away: tell what needs to be told and don't do it in an arbitrary way. There must be order. Whatever order that you put what you are telling in, it should be cohesive and satisfactory. This cohesion is what we call structure.

Draft 1 (Or... Learning What You Are Really Working With)

> "The hardest thing about getting the first draft finished is getting the first draft finished."
>
> ~ David S. Goyer, screenwriter, *The Dark Knight* trilogy, *Man of Steel*

The first draft is both the most fun pass at creating a solo piece and, personally speaking, also the most frustrating. Expect false starts, wrong turns, flights of fancy and so on.

One of the most difficult parts of getting the first draft down on paper is resisting the urge to rewrite as you go along and never actually getting through the whole thing. At least, that is what I have experienced.

The first draft is a first draft, so expect it to be a glorious mess. You have an idea of what happens, but it might still be vague. If you are not sure exactly what happens write THAT down, "I know something like this will happen, but I'm not sure." If you're the only one who can make any sense of it, that's fine. Themes and premise will not do you much good yet. Until you have a first draft to apply it to, these bigger concepts usually take a backseat to more practical details... like what happens (i.e. the plot).

This is one of the reasons I am a fan of traditional plot structure. The simple question of what happens next can be daunting, but if you use structure like scaffolding, you have a framework to work with. You won't get lost (or as easily blocked) if you know where your story needs to go next.

For instance, if you recognize you are at the end of the introduction of your piece, you know something dramatic needs to happen to act as an inciting incident. That, of course, leaves the question of *what* that event is, but at least you know what that event needs to accomplish. If it is the inciting incident it needs to take the main character from the status quo of the first part of your story and thrust him or her into the rising action.

As you work your way through your first draft, just keep going. Trudge through. In my experience the first draft is often a grind. I expect it to be so now, and am pleasantly surprised if, in rare circumstance, things flow smoothly out of my imagination onto the page. In fact, if things go smoothly, it makes me intensely suspect that I am leaving things out or am missing something.

For a monologue-style show that will last between 50 to 55 minutes (i.e. festival length), you can expect to have a single-spaced Word document that spans approximately 20 pages. This is just a ballpark guess, since the pacing of your narrative, the speed of your delivery, the number of technical cues and the amount of "silent" stage bits will inform the final running time as much, if not more than, the text. This first draft will, of course, be edited down later. Over-writing is okay at this stage, too.

When you have the first written version of your show, and only after you have the first fully written version of your show, you will have the opportunity to look at it from different angles. You can take a macro view of the piece, and then, change what needs changing. I think of the first draft like the spaghetti test... throw your script against the wall and see what sticks.

Keep in mind that it is hardest at the beginning. As you finish each draft it becomes easier and, in my experience, more fun. It is the most discouraging and hardest at the beginning. That's why you want to dash through the first draft and get it done with no correcting. Plenty of time to do that later.

You can't begin to improve the story until it is in written form. When a sculptor is starting out he has a slab of stone that he will chisel away at, but the writer-performer does not have that. So the first draft is like creating that slab of stone in the first place. Then the solo performer can start to chip away at.

So, at the risk of sounding like a broken record, here is the take-away of this section: Work your way through an entire draft. Don't go back at all until you're at the end of that first draft. Extensive editing and rewrites will come later.

The Rough Outline

So what is one strategy you can use to help get that first draft banged out? I like to make a rough outline first. Sometimes, I'll even put a bulletin board up on my wall and stick either post-it notes or note cards to it. The note cards have little scene descriptions. The bulletin board is slowly filled in and, like putting down a basic outline, it allows you to see your entire show at a glance.

This sort of "bird's eye view" of your show helps a lot. You can see the whole thing like a snapshot. This gives you an idea of what the overall shape of the piece will be. What is the overall impression the show will leave the audience with? Is it a coherent idea?

Once I have the outline and a basic list of scenes, I start to flesh out those scenes and string everything together. I am building the show from the ground up. Piece by piece, detail by detail, I put the show together like a big puzzle. This eventually is what turns into my first draft.

I will address this more a little later, but this preparation stage is sometimes really extensive, depending on the show. The more prep you do the better your first draft will be. That said, sometimes my outline before starting is really vague simply because I just don't know what happens yet. Or, I don't quite know what exactly I want to say just yet. In these cases, I tend to write a lot. I write to actually figure out what I am trying to articulate. This form of discovery writing is often filled with missteps and backtracking. I have found that this approach takes longer, but can prove to be very rewarding since it favors exploration over execution.

Whether you prefer to do a lot of outlining and prep, or you want to take the long road approach to your first draft, take whatever path fits you and fits the project you are working on.

Let It Percolate... Again

The other thing that I do, and I find that other sorts of creators do as well, is kind of carry the show around in my mind as I am in the process of developing it. The more projects I have done over time, the more this has become sort of automatic. I remember at the beginning, when I first started making solo shows, I had to consciously choose to *think* about my show.

To carry it around in the back of your mind lets your subconscious work on the piece. I find I get ideas and sometimes work out whole sections of a show when I am in the shower in the morning, or driving on the highway or doing basic housework. Any activity that occupies a bit of brain power, but doesn't demand a lot of focus is good for letting your mind wonder and mull stuff over. I have found leisurely walks, drifting into an afternoon nap and bike rides around my neighborhood also serve as good think-about activities.

Sometimes, if I am reading or watching something that is only halfway holding my interest, an idea for the show I am working on will appear.

Where and whenever a thought hits, I quickly record it. I get it down on paper or on Evernote (my note-taking app of choice) via my phone. I also keep note cards in my office, on my bathroom sink and in my car's glove box so I can jot things down real fast. Catch everything. Do not let ideas get away. I even keep a notepad next to the bed so I can capture ideas that hit as I'm falling asleep or as I am just waking up, when the brain is fluid. On rare occasions I even wake in the middle of the night and, coming out of a dream, write down a whole smattering of stuff by the light of my alarm clock. It doesn't always make as much sense in the morning, but at least those thoughts are not gone.

A note about ideas. I have found that the best ones don't come on command. They have to be kind of snuck up on. Or lured in. And they often don't come when it is convenient to record them. Getting a great idea for your show is awesome. Getting a great idea in the shower makes writing that idea down a bit tricky.

I used to think if I had an idea and didn't write it down immediately, it was okay. The idea would surely come back later, especially if it was a good idea. My observation over the years has shown me that it doesn't work that way. Whether the idea is worthwhile or not, it never seems to return. Ideas are fleeting thoughts.

Author Elizabeth Gilbert presented a wonderful TED talk where she explained her belief that creative ideas are disembodied spirits that float through the world and alight on an artist. If the artist is ready to receive the idea, then the idea will stop and inhabit and come through the artist. If the artist is not prepared or aware, then the idea will move on to someone else. I think this is a beautiful concept.

I don't know where ideas come from, but I know that inspiration is not dependable. It can come at odd times or not show up at all. If it appears in the room, it often has to be clutched and wrestled to the ground.

Record any and all ideas or kiss them goodbye.

I call this intangible process "letting it percolate." I let the show kind of float around in my thoughts and let my mind kind of come at it from different angles. I usually let this percolating process happen for several weeks, or at least until I have a nice stack of notes and ideas recorded. The process often continues as the first draft takes shape.

Skip Over Gaps

When you are writing the first draft you might get stuck at some point or another. This happens to me all the time. If I grind to a halt and try to get over whatever is blocking me, I will often lose any and all momentum I might have built up. The flow of ideas is like a shark. If it stops it dies.

To combat this, I will sometimes, particularly in a first draft, just put a little note like "Here X needs to confront Y about the shoes." It would be cryptic if someone else were to glance at my work, but for me it is just a little shorthand note on something I'll need to come back to later.

I will skip that part and go on to the next thing and keep writing. Afterwards, when I get to the end of the draft, I'll go back and fill in the gaps. In a lot of cases, it will be simpler because I have fleshed out a later point. I can kind of go back in and retro-engineer where I need the narrative to go to get to where it ends up.

This, of course, is not always possible.

Sometimes, you don't know where your show will go if you have too many skipped-over gaps. It sort of depends on the nature of the section you are skipping over.

Don't feel pressured to have to complete the whole draft in chronological order. Don't feel like you need to stop and problem solve when you are just trying to get the initial ideas down on paper. Don't mess up your flow.

After you have completed the first draft, you are ready to really see what you are working with. You now have the beginnings of a show on your hands. The next step is getting it up on its feet and hearing it out loud.

CHAPTER 3 – SOUNDING BOARD

Get it in front of people... read it out loud...

Once you have a full first draft you are ready to start forming those initial ideas and rough structure into a cohesive show. Personally, I find this part to be really fun. Trying out what you have on the page and shaping the words and actions into a meaningful presentation happens in a series of cumbersome steps, but these steps need not be frustrating (or at least not as frustrating as putting together the first draft).

The first thing I usually do after finishing the first draft is to put the script down for several days. This little gap gives me enough space to come back to the script fresh and see it with new eyes.

I usually do one more thing before starting rewrites. I read the show out loud. I do this a couple of times. I literally read it out loud to myself. Later on in the process, before I start rehearsing the piece, I'll read the script out loud to others. These readings out loud are not so much to entertain, but to examine. Since I will be the person eventually performing the piece, I read the script out loud to get a preliminary hearing of what it will sound like coming out of my mouth.

Throughout the first draft process, I will have gotten really close to the piece. By reading the script out loud, I can check that the narrative is clear and there aren't big plot holes. I can check to see if the characters have clear motivations and progress through the story as they need to.

There seems to be a certain blindness one can develop when in the middle of some project, especially something especially creative. Sometimes what happens in our minds doesn't make it out and onto the page like we think it does. Think back to when you had to write essays in high school. If you ever turned a paper into a teacher and were surprised when you received your grade back, you will know what I am talking about. What you were thinking is not what ended up on your paper and your teacher probably loved telling you how he or she was "not a mind reader."

So, reading the script out loud is a chance to make sure that what is in your head makes sense once it is down on the page. It is also a good idea to read the script out loud to someone else.

A sounding board is a literal screen or board placed behind or over a pulpit, rostrum, or platform to reflect the sound of a speaker's voice forward. For our purposes, a sounding board is also the term used to describe a person or a group of people whose reactions and impressions of your show can be used as a sort of test of the show's validity. These first reactions can give us a bit of insight on the clarity of the show and the likeliness of its impact and success before it is made public.

The sounding board phase comes after you have a full first draft completed. This is the laboratory phase in which the piece is tested and tested again. I will address using others as sounding boards more in

Chapter 5. Reading the piece out loud from the first draft onward is part of the next step… rewrites.

CHAPTER 4 – REWRITES

Rewrites are a must. I wish I could, with a straight face, tell you it is possible to stop at your first draft and put that up on stage. No more work needed. That is a quaint theory with absolutely zero practical or anecdotal evidence to support it. In fact, as a life philosophy I do not believe in first drafts. People that turn in first drafts of things deserve whatever they get.

I teach college students and I tell them if they ever turn in the first draft of something, not just in my class, but in any class, they very much deserve a "first draft grade." I then tell them if they choose to be a "first draft person" then I will silently judge them and pity their life choices."

Rewrites are exactly what they sound like. You will rewrite parts of or, possibly, even the entire show. This is the editing phase.

This process could take a day or two or up to a few weeks in my experience. It depends on how complex your show is, how much rewriting needs to be done and how much time you have to dedicate to the continuing development of your show.

The goal of rewrites is to ensure that your show is clear, stage-worthy, well-paced and has the impact you want it to have.

A lot of the rewriting process is cutting or moving around scenes or episodes, making sure each bit of the piece serves the narrative as well as the message you are trying to get across and, most especially, that the piece will engage the audience from start to finish.

Keep what works and throw out or reshape what doesn't. Here are a few tips from my own experience that I have found that may help as you make your way through rewrites.

The first thing I would recommend would be to actually print out your script. This will sound pretty rudimentary to some, but as the world moves more and more away from the printed page and onto screens, this is worth mentioning.

A paper print-out of the entire script will allow you to mark up the pages with a pencil or pen. The editing I do on my first draft print-outs includes many spelling corrections, additions, clarifications, questions I need to answer in future drafts, and so on.

It sounds dreadfully analogue, but I do recommend trying it out. If you usually do all corrections on a screen, then you might be surprised at how tactile and useful editing on an actual piece of paper is. I find it especially useful in that I can physically carry around the script and make additions and edits at random times, not just when I'm sitting down at my computer or tablet. All I need is a pen or pencil.

My first draft is inevitably covered with marginalia, little arrows connecting revisions and new thoughts, as well as lots and lots of cross-outs.

I end up collecting these marked-up drafts in a binder. Any notes I make as well as any "journal" entries also go in this binder. I call it the Project Binder and I'll discuss it more later.

Work in chunks

Looking at the script as a whole can be a little overwhelming. There can seem to be so many moving parts in your narrative that it may seem impossible to keep everything straight. To counteract this, I often work in chunks.

The "chunks" of the script roughly correspond with the five act structure I laid out earlier. I take the first chunk of the piece which is usually the opening episode or hook (I'll touch on this more in a bit), the introduction with its necessary exposition, status quo, establishing of the setting and so on. Then, I'll move on to the inciting incident and then to rising action and so on. As I make changes, I will leave myself little notes to fix later in the story, or I will go back and make a correction or clarification or addition if I change something later in the story that needs some early set up. I look at the piece as a collection of "chunks" and do my best to revise each, in turn, then ultimately, after working my way through each chunk, go back to look over the script as a whole.

The rewriting process does not seem so daunting when I am only working with three or four pages at a time. I use this "chunks" approach when I get to the rehearsal stage as well. More on the rehearsal process later.

One of the main things I focus on during the rewriting process is to look for plot holes. Story logic has to be maintained. Audiences will pick up on things that don't make sense. I am always bugged in movies when a plot point happens and I sit there thinking,

"Wait. Why don't they just do this?" I am super sensitive to the plot making sense.

Sometimes the character makes choices that don't make sense… initially. Or at least, the character himself doesn't know why he made a decision in such a way. If this is the case, I will acknowledge it. I will have the character realize that he or she doesn't know what is motivating them. They are as perplexed as the audience is. I find this usually works better if I allow the show to draw attention to itself if something seems confusing on the surface. Often, the motivation makes sense later, with more context, but if it doesn't initially add up narratively, you can bet the audience will be thinking, "Wait. Why did the character do that?"

If you find areas where things don't quite add up, concentrate on fixing those as you go from draft to draft. Rest assured, the audience will notice if there is a break down in story logic, a character inconsistency or a weird tonal shift.

Another thing to keep in mind as you work through the improvement process is to remember you are writing a piece of theatre. You aren't writing a novel or a poem or an essay. You are writing something that you will eventually perform for an audience. There's an old playwriting axiom that it is always better to show than it is to tell. I mostly agree with this. Here's an example…

You could have a scene where a character is afraid of something. This character could come on to stage and look out at the audience and say, "I am so scared." This is one way to establish that the character is frightened.

On the other hand, you could have the lights dim on stage, then have the character run onto the stage at full speed, frantic and sweating. The character dives under a bed then peers out at the audience wild-eyed and shaking, holding a crucifix in one hand and a string of garlic in the other.

Both of these scenarios indicate that the character is afraid, but one if simply much more theatrical (therefore stronger) than the other. Notice the stronger version doesn't even use dialogue. As you are rewriting just keep in mind that you are crafting a piece of theatre and not simply a stand-alone monologue or simple story.

Above, I said, "I *mostly* agreed" with the Show, Don't Tell expression. I believe a stronger way to look at it might be that one should Show *and* Tell. Theatre is a pretty verbal medium. At least, it is verbal compared with, say, television and film, which are considerably more visual art forms. Tell what you need to, show what you can.

Don't indulge in too many descriptions. What I mean is, unless it is really important for context, do not spend a bunch of stage time *describing* things to the audience, particularly people or environments. Novels, short stories and other kinds of literature are better for using long descriptive passages. On stage, the actor can show that the room is cold, or that a character is nervous. Character traits can be acted. Descriptions can add context, but too much can really slow down the plot. A stage show is something that can be presented in a dynamic way, so then, present it in that dynamic way. Give the audience enough information to keep up, but try not to hold their hands.

Speaking of the audience, keep them in mind as you rewrite. Ultimately, you will be up on stage presenting this show to rooms of people who will, ideally, have paid to see you. What do you want them to see? How do you want them to experience the production?

Make your show compelling. This seems like straightforward advice, but I have seen a lot of solo shows that are, for the most part really strong and engaging, but somehow have one or a few parts that are just slow. Or boring. Or overly loaded with exposition. Or are obviously filler because the performer couldn't think of a good way to transition from one part of their story to another.

There shouldn't be any parts that could be described as "filler." Make sure you keep the piece taut. An acting teacher of mine many years ago described the relationship between the performer on stage and the audience listening out in the house as a musical metaphor. He said to pretend there was a string connecting the performer to the audience and that as long as the string is kept tight, then it could be strummed and produce vibrations. It can be "played." The mark of a great performer is how well he or she played this "connection" between the actor and spectators. However, if the string slackens, the reverberations stop. No reverberation means no music, no connection.

Playwright David Mamet once said very bluntly that the audience really only wants one thing. It wants to know what happens next. I think the audience wants more than that from a theatre production, but Mamet makes a strong point. Just like in life, we are hard-wired to want to know what happens next. Aristotle famously said that the greatest pleasure a human can want for is to know the truth, to gain knowledge. Humans want to know things. We want to know the score. We want to know about those around us, about the world around us, about ourselves. We want to know where we have been and where we are and where we are going. This urge to know is why the dopamine hit is so strong when we scroll through social media. We want to know what's up.

In a theatre production the audience wants to know what happens in the next moment. This tension and anticipation is part of what makes that string of connection tight. That is what makes the show compelling. If the audience gets ahead of your narrative the enjoyment shrinks to the shallow level of "Aha, I knew it." If you get too far ahead of your audience, if you lose them, then they will grown upset, confused and disappointed that they can't follow what is happening.

As you work through rewrites, remember to make your show compelling. Seduce, frighten, cajole, amuse, or touch their heart-strings. Do what you need to do to retain your audience's interest, to compel them to keep watching. Make them want to know what happens next and then deliver the next thing and move on to the next thing after that.

One way to keep your story compelling is to make sure it has sufficient conflict. In real life, we often avoid conflict if we can. My wife, for instance, will go to great lengths not to get into an argument (with people other than me). In the theatre, conflict is a good thing. Our characters have to strive to get what they want and there should be things in their way. The more they have to struggle the better. Audiences relate with characters who struggle. Everyone on Earth believes they struggle, no matter where he or she falls on the socio-economic spectrum. Wall Street bankers all the way to homeless people living on the streets… everyone believes they struggle The thing is, quite often we, as people, really do struggle. But no one has ever come along and stated, "Yeah, I don't want anything else. I'm good. Got it all figured out. Yeah, across the board, on everything, I'm good."

If your character wants something and then gets it too easily, then your story is probably unsatisfying to watch. This is a particular problem when a performer pulls too explicitly from real life. The performer might argue that the character in their show, usually a thinly fictionalized version of themselves, actually took a certain approach to solve a problem, so it doesn't need to be theatrical or dynamic. Since that is how something played out in real life, then it should get a pass on stage. This is a stupid argument.

The audience only sees your theatre version of events. Make that version exciting, whether it plays out the same way it did in real life or not.

The other reason a solo performer may avoid conflict in his or her script is because it is challenging to write. Just like in real life, it is way easier to get into trouble than it is to get out of trouble. So, whatever dilemma you put your characters in, you also have to get them back out of it. Sometimes, a would-be playwright will think that the whole thing would be simpler if you didn't throw so much at the characters in the first place. But this, too, is unexciting to watch.

It keeps the stakes low. Avoiding conflict is just lazy writing.

Opening Hook

The first image, scene or statement of your show should hook the audience. Much like the first sentence of a novel, the first thing the audience sees in your solo show should be dynamic. It should make the spectators ask, "What happens next?" or "Whoa! That's cool."

Take a moment as you work through the rewrites to give special consideration to the opening moments of your piece. How can you set the tone or mood? Does it engage the audience and make them want to keep watching?

I often start my shows with an arresting visual stage picture or some sort of conflict. I start my show *Cyrano A-Go-Go*, about the 1897 play *Cyrano de Bergerac,* with the line:

"So, early in the play – Act I – of *Cyrano de Bergerac*, a naïve fop challenges Cyrano to a duel. In the history of literary wrong moves, this is definitely right at the top."

I then enact the Ballad of the Duel from Rostand's play, playing both sides of the sword fight while composing the "je touché" poem.

Come out strong, avoid the mundane or lackluster. Hook your audience right from the start.

It is possible to simply come out on stage and begin speaking, but what is said should be arresting, funny, devastating or unique right away.

Theme is purpose

Another thing I focus on during rewrites is clarifying the theme of the piece. I start with a rough idea, but after the first draft I often find many more opportunities to strengthen the thematic thru line.

I have observed that the theme becomes the purpose for the piece. As I make my way from one draft to another, I look for ways to bring out the thematic elements more and more. The theme, of course, becomes what the piece is really about. How can the characters strengthen the themes? How can the structure or the setting strengthen the themes?

Often, I will identify a big over-arching theme and with it smaller themes that fill the piece. For instance, my show *Robert's Eternal Goldfish* is about a misanthropic man who becomes the unlikely custodian of a magical goldfish. The goldfish haunts him into becoming a (slightly) better person. The main theme concerns the self-destructive effects of misanthropy. However, during the course of the play - although to lesser degrees - other themes surface. The show offers insights on disconnection in contemporary life, the power of the artist, the effects of dreams on real life, the disappearance of good customer service, overcoming trauma, the benefits of reaching out for help with problems of mental health and lots of other thematic concepts.

As you identify concepts worth exploring you will begin to see what your show is really about. A theme will appear. Then multiple thematic elements will begin to fill out and underscore that bigger theme. A strong theme will give your show have importance and purpose.

As you develop the piece, the theme will become clearer and clearer. Be sure to pay attention once it presents itself and then do what you can to strengthen it.

A Word About Separating the Development Process into Distinct Drafts.

Label your individual drafts. I mean, on your computer, do not save over an earlier draft with the same name, but instead save the newer draft with a slightly different name. For instance, I label my drafts either by date or my draft number.

I will title the document "Name of Script – Draft 1" or "Name of Script – Early Feb 2021" so I can keep all the separate versions, well, separate. The next draft would be named "Name of Script – Draft 2" or "Name of Script – Late Feb 2021" and so on. Keeping each individual draft seems so straightforward, and such a small thing, but this was a lesson I learned the hard way. Early on, I would just save over former drafts and then if I wanted to bring back in something I had put in an earlier draft, I had to try to remember it and retype it. Save yourself the head-ache.

Since I am writing this all down in a book, I have done my best to codify the steps I normally take to create a show. Typically I do a first draft, take a break for a while, then come back and rewrite another few drafts before I begin to put the piece up on its feet.

In reality this process is amorphous and fluid. I sometimes, depending on the show, will do an immense amount of preparation leading up to the first draft. I will try to recognize any embedded structural problems and work out fixes before I even start writing the first draft itself. I make an outline of the order of the scenes or episodes and then I try to make the first draft as great as I can. This ensures I get the story and its structure pretty solid really early on. In these cases, I usually only need another pass or two at the script before I put it up on its feet.

The map that I have laid out in the previous few chapters of separate and deliberate steps is just one way to do it and the way that has worked for me in the past.

The goal stays the same regardless of how you approach it. Turn the rough idea into a first draft, then rewrite as needed to make the script stage-worthy.

Ultimately, follow your own organic process. I am only offering possibilities here. Once again, there is not a perfect approach, only what works for you.

CHAPTER 5 – REHEARSING

Get it in Front of (A Few) People

I have found the fastest and most enlightening way to develop a show from the first draft stage to getting it towards its final form is to read the piece out loud in front of people. This can happen in several different ways. Here we return to the sounding board concept I discussed earlier.

The first person I usually read my work out loud to is my wife, Ruth. I only read her about ten minutes at a time as that is about as long as I can reliably expect her to stand still and patiently listen to me. As I read, with the script in front of me and pencil in hand, I will jot notes in the margins of things to look back at. I will also catch any points where I worded something in a weird way. I also, on a practical note, try to fix spelling and basic grammar mistakes, since I *see* the words in a new way when I am reading them out loud.

Over a day or two, I will read the entire show to Ruth. She is good about asking for clarification when something is confusing. She is also good about asking leading questions that make me think about the piece from different perspectives.

This seeing the piece from alternate perspectives that I had not considered is a bonus that is specific to my wife. While this is often irksome in other aspects of our life together (arguments are difficult beyond the usual reasons simply because within minutes we are both, inevitably, talking about different things), it is kind of beneficial when I am reading her something new that I am working on. She will get fixated on a specific word, or image or some angle that I might not have paid enough attention to up to that point. Often, I will wonder if she has understood the wider point because she will have latched on to something in a way that is very laser focused and from a completely different perspective from what I could have even imagined. If you have someone like this in your life, count it as a blessing and use their weird way of seeing things to make your work better.

Memorize

So, the tedious part comes before the really fun part in rehearsals. Before you can play around with characterizations and pacing and stage pictures and everything else, you need to know your script forwards and backwards. You need to know your narrative so well you can recite it the same way you could recite the Pledge of Allegiance every morning back when you were in elementary school (that is, you know, if you went to an American public school growing up).

According to Austrian neurophysiologist and philosopher Dr. John C. Eccles: "When you learn anything, a pattern of neurons forming a chain is set up in your brain tissue. This chain or electrical pattern is your brain's way of remembering. The electrical pathways within the nervous system insure the repetition of habitual tasks."

So, repetition is the key. I wish I could give you some bullet-proof shortcuts for memorizing your script. Unfortunately, I have yet to find anything as simple and foolproof as straight up repetition. Just go over and over your script, word by word, sentence by sentence and then paragraph by paragraph. In this way, you literally "wire" it into your brain.

Depending on how complex the script is, I can usually memorize about a page to two pages in a day. Sometimes it is more and sometimes less. Progress usually depends on my mood and my ability to focus that day. If I have been memorizing a lot in a short span of time, I pick things up quicker. Memory is a muscle. It gets stronger with use.

Depending on what else I have going on in my life at the time, an initial rehearsal day for me - especially at the beginning of the rehearsal process - is often split into two or three sessions. Each session lasts 45 minutes to an hour. I try to go for short intense bouts of focus and memorizing. I'll talk more about some tips to improve your focus in just a bit.

I start at the beginning of the script, on page one, and make my way through, page by page, until I make to the end. For a normal festival-length show, without rushing, it usually takes a week and a half to two weeks to get the whole thing hardwired reliably into my brain.

The nice part I have found, at least in my own experience, is that the task gets a little easier the further into the script I get. After a week of concentrated work, my brain seems to become adjusted to the rote execution of learning the lines verbatim off the page. I also absorb the nuances of the story as I go along, so the narrative itself gets hardwired into my brain. As I get to know the plot, point by point, as well as the changes the characters go through, beat by beat, everything starts to fall into place. I recognize where the story is going and all the little twists and turns it takes and this seems to help with the rank memorization as well.

I read the sentence I am about to say very carefully, then say it out loud. Then I say it again. And again. And so on. I repeat a single line a dozen times or more until it is locked, word by exact word, into my memory. I pay special attention to how the sentence relates to the previous sentence and how it sets up the next sentence.

Repetition and Concentration

Perhaps someone somewhere has come up with a shortcut, but I have yet to find a way to get around simply repeating, out loud, the lines until it is in my brain and body. I find that memorizing is a tedious, but necessary part of the process. Slowly working the words and what they mean, bit by bit, into your muscle memory can seem to take forever, but it is an important part of the process.

I find that memorizing kind of works in phases, at least for me. The first phase is going word by word, reading and focusing on it, then sort of getting my mouth to remember the feel of saying the words.

The next phase is both saying the words and also seeing the text in my mind. What I mean by this is that I see the page of text in my mind as I am going along. I know if something I am saying is in the script at the bottom of the page or at the top.

The last phase is being so familiar with the script that I can recite it with hardly any effort and at a drop of a hat. By this point, I have been over the script, out loud, more times than I can count. I no longer "see" it in my head, but simply hear it as I am saying it. I know the parts of the narrative and how they fit together. I have both a macro view of the story as a whole, but also a full grasp of all the little details, too.

It takes a lot of effort, a lot of focus and usually a lot of time to get to that final phase of memorization. Over time, I have found that there are a few things that help me while memorizing. I offer these tips to you, with the caveat there are many ways to skin a cat. What works for me might not necessarily work for you.

How to memorize... Or, at least, how I do it.

Look at the page. Read and absorb the words. Then look away. It doesn't matter where you look, just don't look back at the page yet. Sometimes it helps if you have a blank wall to look at or an uncluttered part of the room. Let your eyes soften their focus. Now say the words out loud. Then look back at the page and check that you got the words correct. If you are off a bit, try again. Do this little look away and back test until you can say it out loud correctly a few times in a row.

Do this for each sentence in the script. Some sentences will absorb more quickly than others. When you have made your way through a paragraph or two, or maybe a scene, then go back and review it. If you can make your way through the collection of sentences a few times without messing up, then move on. In this way, just proceed through the whole script, back tracking to review what you have learned periodically.

The key is to stay focused on what you are doing. Memorizing is not a multitask activity. This is also why it is best to avoid distractions as much as possible. Every time someone interrupts your rehearsal, every time the phone rings with some notification or another, you are pulled out of the process. And every time you are pulled out of the process you have to basically start all over again on whatever you were immediately focused on.

Attention spans are just that… a span of time when you can focus all your energy on a particular task. Without focusing our attention our minds tend to wander to the past or future (instead of staying in the present), negative thoughts or boredom. But staying focused is difficult, especially nowadays.

I am born of the generation that straddled analogue and digital. I remember operating in the world before the internet, smart phones, steaming services and social media. As I have adapted to the world around me as it currently is, I can attest, diminishing attention spans is a real thing. I have grown use to consuming "content" in small bite-size chunks. From news to entertainment to communications with others around me, I have become noticeably aware that my mind wants to move on to something else faster and more impatiently than it used to. So, when I say staying focused is difficult, I understand that it is especially so nowadays. But focusing is a skill. It can be regained over time the same way it can be diminished over time.

If you find you have a hard time focusing on memorization and rehearsals, first give yourself a break. The world you live in strives to shorten and exploit your attention span. Next, purposefully work on sticking with the things you need to concentrate on. It will gradually get easier to get your mind to center in on what you want it to.

This may seem like a suggestion out of left field, but I would highly recommend a good night's sleep. Good and plentiful sleep is a must when you are trying to commit lots of pages of text to memory. Memorizing takes focus and attention, and you don't want to be battling against your own energy levels to summon it. I recall when I was in college how I'd wait until the end of the day to sit down to study for a test the next day and slowly, but inevitably, drift off right there at the desk, nose down in my notes. I just couldn't rally the mental energy I needed at that point in the day.

I did better when I called it a night at a reasonable time and then got up earlier the next morning to cram, er, I mean study. Getting enough sleep doesn't seem like something I should need to mention, but it is one of those under-the-radar things that can make putting together your show way harder than it needs to be.

As you memorize and understand what the script is saying, take advantage of this point during rehearsals to question your script. As you run the show pay attention to where it lags, where things perhaps don't make as much sense as they need to, or even that a part now seems like filler now that you have it up on your feet. This part of the process is wonderful for discovering just what your script is and how you want it to come across to audiences.

This last part of the memorization period, as I have the show up on its feet is one of the more fun parts for me. It really is a point of discovery. And that is good, because soon, it will be time to batten everything down. You will hopefully come out with a watertight script as you go into tech rehearsals. You will be done goofing around with it. It will be memorized. You will move into the final parts of rehearsing the show. The next stop after this will be performing it… for people.

It is My Own Show. Why do I Need to Memorize?

Before I get entirely ahead of myself, there's a practical reason for getting off-book as soon as you can. It is difficult to block your show (i.e. set the movements around the stage) with the script still in your hand. With your eyes buried in your script it just makes it physically harder to fully perform the show.

The fun part, at least for me, is making discoveries during rehearsals. Messing around with pacing and characterizations, blocking and stage pictures all comes after you commit the text to memory. You can't get to the good stuff until after you handle the rather technical and dry part of the process: memorizing the script.

The other reason I believe memorizing is important is because you may be tempted to rewrite the piece on its feet during performance. I am very guilty of this, thinking that me-in-the-present is smarter, more witty and just plain better than the me-in-the-past that spent weeks fine-tuning a well-written script. This is rarely the case. I will rationalize this by telling myself, especially during early performances, that I am "trying stuff out" in front of the audience. The drawbacks are two-fold. First, the audiences are sort of cheated out of a full, excellent performance. Over the years, this has come to bother me more and more. It is unfair to use paying audiences for tinkering around with your show. It is disrespectful. Your early audiences already get a lesser show than later audiences who see your show once you grown into it. I will touch on this respect for the audience a little more later.

Anyway, sometimes in the early performances of my early shows, I gave in to the moment and I would ad-lib or do a little on-my-feet edit. As an experienced improviser as well as the author of the work, I felt justified in changing whatever I wanted wherever I wanted. The problem with rewriting in performance is that it messes up the timing. As a performer you stay in your head instead of staying in your body, in the room and in the moment. You may also throw off the tech person if you start messing around with the lines.

Ruth, my wife, was my board op (that is short for sound and light board operator) for me as I toured my first show, *Chop*. During tech rehearsals she would be so tight, but during shows she would sometimes be slow on cues. As the person on stage, I would notice, but I let it go for several shows. I figured that she was just making tiny mistakes or was just off here and there. I finally brought it up after one of the shows partway through a fringe festival run. Ruth explained that she had missed some cue lines here and there because I had changed how I was saying the lines. The fact that I continued to change the lines throughout, or slightly rearrange parts of the show, was playing havoc with her hitting the sound and light cues at the proper time. In fact, she explained, it was only because she was so familiar with the show already that she was able to jump in and hit the cues even close to when they needed to happen. I was, in essence, sabotaging my own show by messing around with the text while performing in front of audiences.

Before I am off the subject, there is one more reason to memorize your show. You memorize your show because it is what professionals do. Only amateurs feel they can wing it. If you want to come off like a clueless, unprepared dilettante then be that person who didn't make the effort to memorize their own show before showing it to audiences. It is lazy. It shows lack of integrity. It is also hugely disrespectful to the audience as well as to your own material.

The takeaway here is to respect your show, respect your tech support, respect yourself as a performer and respect the audience. To do this, stick with the script. Do the work. Memorize the piece that you wrote and then perform it as written.

Director or No Director

Some soloists work without a director. For some this seems inconceivable. Unless you are already incredibly experienced in the theatre (and have directing experience of your own) I usually advise new solo performers to work with a director. A director of a solo show does the same thing a director does in a traditional theatre production. They serve as an outside eye and help guide the performer in making discoveries, creating stage pictures, keeping the show well-paced, insure clarity and help in setting up technical requirements.

When I was performing my first solo show *Chop*, I worked with a director named Andrew Merkel. He and I met about a half a dozen times and he asked me really good questions about my script. He also helped me block out the show so I wasn't just standing in one place the whole time.

Since *Chop,* I have often worked without a director. My goal was always to become a one-man show in every since of the word (or as close as I could get to that phrase). However, I will always owe Andrew a debt of gratitude. I don't think I had the confidence to get on stage alone with that first show. Everything felt overwhelming and I felt I needed a director. Having Andrew help me through the process was a great aid, not only to my own sense of can-I-do-this, but to the show itself. Andrew saw things I hadn't thought of, especially since I was in the eye of the storm, so to speak. He was invested in the show. His name was on it, too, and he wanted it to go well.

Nowadays, I usually do not work with a director when developing a new solo show. This practice has, admittedly, been difficult and it demands much more attention. It is another hat I have to wear. I will sometimes video record rehearsals to get an outside eye on the show. This is particularly helpful with pacing, since I find this is one of the hardest things to gage for myself as a performer. I think the shows are still fine (I have an extensive background in directing), but I have noticed one outstanding trade-off. Since that first show *Chop*, my shows have been nowhere as technically extensive. There are less light and sound cues, less set design, and less overall movement around the stage. While I can rationalize this as moving towards a tighter, more essential, more minimal approach, the truth of the matter is, I can only do so much on my own. The theatricality now comes from the storytelling and characterizations more than the blocking, tech and scenery... because it has to.

Speaking of Tech and Scenery

After you have memorized your piece and set the script, you are ready to consider the technical side of your show. This includes lighting changes, sound cues, specialty props, slide projections and so on. You know, the stuff theatre often includes.

I have a few specific suggestions when you are working on the "tech" for your show. First, consider where you are going to do your show. If you plan to take it around to fringe festivals and tour extensively with your show, you may consider reducing your technical requirements to a minimum. Consider the many places you may take your show. A lot of festivals offer little more than makeshift platforms as stages. More on touring a little later. On the other hand, if you plan to take your show to fully outfitted venues such as city municipal performing arts centers or regional theatres, then you can deck your show out a bit more. The more technical requirements you have in your show the more it will cost to transport it, the longer it will take to set cues in each venue and the more you have to keep track of. I'm not saying to purposely limit yourself, but just be aware of the logistics of extensive technical requirements.

Next, I highly recommend you specifically keep notes about tech needs as you rehearse your piece. Every time you have a thought like, "a sound effect would be great right here…" or, "The lights should dim at this moment," write it down. Then, go through and write the cues in your script where they need to go. Some solo performers I know have brought in stage managers to help with this process.

Hiring a local stage manager is not a bad idea, especially if your show has more than a few lighting and sound cues. It is even possible to hire a stage manager or board op in the cities where you go to perform.

Once you have all your cues gathered in your script, you will need to make a master cue list as well. A master cue list is exactly what it sounds like. It is a spreadsheet that lists out what the cue is (sound, light or something else), what page it is on and during what line of the text it happens. A lot of performers don't bother to do this, and if you only have two or three cues perhaps it is unnecessary, but if you have a lot of sound and light cues it is a good practice to get into. Also, your future board ops will thank you for it.

One more thing I need to advise about the technical part of your show is to really question whether you need as many sound cues, lighting changes, costume changes, props, set pieces and so on. Just because you think up a cool bit of business or lighting trick or sound effect, that doesn't automatically mean it should be included. By all means, try it out in rehearsal if possible, but always evaluate whether the tech element truly adds to the show. If it is just a "meh" moment or, worse, distracts from the themes, pacing, characters and story you are telling then cut it and go with a simpler choice.

One last word about unnecessary technical stuff. Remember, everything you don't do yourself on stage is basically out of your control. If the lights don't change the way they should or when they should, there is very little you can do about in the middle of a performance. If the sound cue doesn't come in when it should or is too low a volume, then you will just have to suffer through. Too many slide projections take the audiences' eyes off of you. I sat through a show once where the performer literally left the stage for a minute and half to do a costume change (which, in my opinion, was not even necessary to her show) while the whole audience sat in polite, and rather confused, silence looking at an empty stage. Make sure whatever technical elements you use in your show genuinely help the show and don't take away from it.

Setting a Rehearsal Schedule

One potential problem I see happen with solo performances that I don't observe as much in traditional productions is what may be referred to as a certain *casualness* with the rehearsal schedules. There seems to be this thought that most of the heavy lifting has been done once the show is created and roughly staged. This is 180 degrees incorrect, but the notion still exists. The heavy lifting has just started.

In a traditional multi-actor show, the director makes the rehearsal schedule. He or she plans out several weeks of meetings with the cast to practice and hone the play. He or she works backwards from the opening date and calculates how much can be done in any single rehearsal session, what the parameters of the show call for that might demand extra time and attention (Is there singing? Physical bits of business? Special props?), and so on. The director then has the stage manager contact the actors with the schedule and informs them when they, personally, will be called. It is all neat and organized in most cases.

Solo shows, especially ones without a director, are not usually like that. It is on the performer, him or herself, to set the rehearsal schedule. Theoretically, the performer knows themselves. They know how fast they can memorize, how focused they can be, and how much progress can be done in each session leading up to the first performance of the show. But like a lot of theories, in practice, stuff rarely works out as perfectly as it does on paper.

Life happens. Some days the performer is tired, or sore or just doesn't feel like rehearsing. If the rehearsal space is his or her own apartment or house, does the presence of other people who live there come into play?

Since I have fallen prey to most of the challenges that can confront an independent solo performer, my advice is to sit down and really calculate out what sort of time you will need to set aside for rehearsals and then add several more sessions as "cushion."

Let's say you have an hour-long show, roughly 20-ish pages of script, and it is predominantly first person monologue. Maybe there is one or two bits that have to be worked out with musical cues and a specialized prop (maybe a flashlight that you use at one point to illuminate your face campfire-style as the rest of the stage is plunged into complete darkness).

So, let's say you can memorize about a page and half a day. So about fifteen rehearsals, give or take, are needed for the initial memorization phase. Let's say each rehearsal is an intense two-hour session. That's thirty hours. Then you calculate you'll run the show in real time about a dozen times to get the pacing down and work out the bits, like the one with the flashlight.

An hour-long show times twelve is twelve hours, but usually you'll run it twice in each rehearsal. So, six hours and some change on "run-thrus" is set aside. We are up to a thirty-eight hour rehearsal process. Now add two or three more sessions as a "cushion" to account for late starts, life interruptions and general falling behind.

You can expect, realistically, that to get your hour-long show fully on its feet from the page to the stage to take approximately forty two hours. Now sit down with a calendar and budget those rehearsal hours out over the appropriate number of weeks.

You could do fourteen three hour sessions which would be a three-hour rehearsal every day for two weeks. Or maybe spread it out over three or four weeks, depending on what your own obligations are in life.

I usually average about three weeks for rehearsing most of my shows and plan to be up to performance level at least a week or so before I have to perform it the first time for an audience. In that week I usually do a line-through at least once a day to keep it fresh in my mind (often I do this while I drive around running errands). The "cushion" week allows me to become really comfortable with the new piece so it is not such a run-up to performance and I don't get too nervous with opening night jitters.

Of course, this three-week process plus a cushion week is an ideal scenario. I have also stressed out because I left myself too little time in the past. It is more of an art than a science.

What I am getting at is that it will take a while initially. Or I should say, it will take a while to do it *right*. Just embrace and accept this. Unfortunately, I have encountered a lot of performers who rush the rehearsal process, either not putting enough forethought into the process or not taking it seriously enough, or just letting life get in the way and allowing that to be a rationalization why the performance of their show sucks.

Worse than cramming or rationalizing, I have encountered a handful of solo performers who have just winged it completely. Either they horribly under-rehearsed or perhaps they did not rehearse at all.

While one of these performers was actually pretty decent, the result has been overwhelmingly underwhelming. Shows, and the performers who do them, end up never rising anywhere near their potential. In fact, they often just flat out suck.

The good news is that I have found that solo shows, like other plays, are front-loaded. Once you do the work up front, the maintenance of the show is relatively simple. So, allow for a long enough rehearsal process and don't make it hard on yourself having to scramble. Remember, art is a process. And it should be a good, challenging, enjoyable process.

It May Seem Lonely

I don't need to spend much time on this because it is self-evident, but I figured I should at least mention that working on a one-person show can sometimes be lonely. This is especially true if you are accustomed to the camaraderie of the rehearsal process of a traditional play with a multi-character cast.

You are the driver of the process. It is up to you to stay upbeat, enthusiastic and moving forward. I won't sugar-coat it. Sometimes, that is difficult.

Sometimes, I feel like I am just yelling into the wind for a long time until I get my show in front of an audience. It can sometimes make the process seem longer than it actually is. I don't think that feeling of isolation is all that unique to me. I think it is something a lot of solo performers struggle with to varying degrees. This is particularly apparent if you are not working with a director or some other kind of collaborator. For me, it is not soul-crushing, but I am conscious of feeling a bit lonesome from time to time when I am rehearsing a solo show.

If you find that you are having these feelings as well, don't worry. I think it is a pretty normal feeling. Also, it will pass. Once you start getting your show in front of audiences, those lonesome feelings dissipate.

Here's some take-aways: pay attention to the cues that you actually need. Be sure to budget your rehearsal time and don't put yourself in a lurch.

Blocking – Don't Just Stand Around

I find one of the more challenging aspects of putting together a solo show is generating interesting blocking and engaging stage pictures for myself within the show's context. The word *blocking*, as I referenced earlier, is a theatre term that simply means where actors move on the stage.

I see a lot of shows where the performer just stands in the middle of the space, like a stand-up comedian. This is understandable, since there is often not a very extensive amount of scenery to interact with. There is also an absence of other actors on stage to address and play off of. In fact, more often than not the solo performer is speaking directly to the audience, so faces that one direction the entire time.

I try to find ways to make the show more visually dynamic. I have found the simplest way to make sure I'm not just sitting in one place, or standing around in the middle of the stage, is to put several different "areas" around the playing space.

For instance, in the show *Chop* that I keep referencing, I made several areas or zones. I had a chair over on stage left, angled slightly inward at a diagonal. I put a little table on the right hand side of the stage. I also made two sideshow banners that hung upstage as makeshift backdrops. I used the space between the banners as a sort of entry way. I could also walk behind them or peek around them.

The last area was a bit downstage at the center of the set. Different scenes took place in different areas of the stage.

For instance, the table became a birthday party, a kitchen table, a buffet table at a cocktail party and so on. The chair represents an office cubicle, a rocking chair on a porch, and a hospital bed among other locales. Here's what those areas look like from above. The gray circles are the areas that represent different environments, or playing areas in *Chop*, where I would stop and perform scenes:

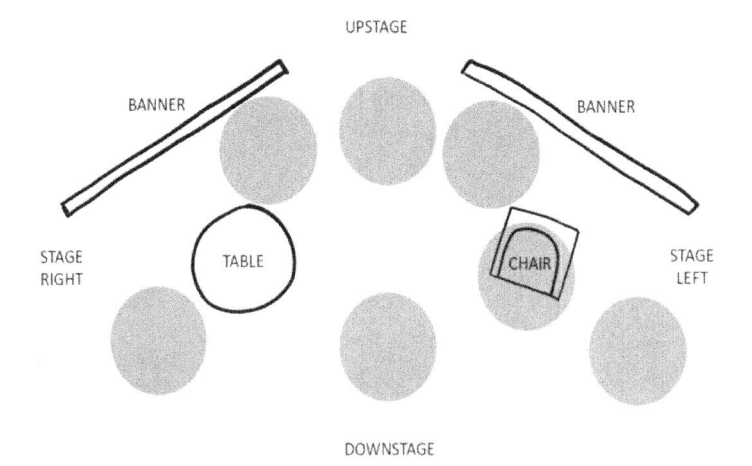

```
                          UPSTAGE

          BANNER                        BANNER
                      ○         ○
                 ○                   ○
                                   ┌──┐
   STAGE        ╭───╮             │CHAIR│      STAGE
   RIGHT       │TABLE│             └──┘        LEFT
                ╰───╯
                      ○         ○

                         DOWNSTAGE
```

Besides using parts of the stage as playing areas, I also used the spaces between set pieces as thresholds and walkways. For instance, Andy, the director, would have me walk around the table and "step into" a new environment.

Here's a look at the stage as a whole for *Chop*. In this photo I am standing in the downstage center position, but you can see the chair and table and banners on the stage. I should note, originally, the sideshow banners were full color. These seemed distracting, however, once I saw a few production photos of early performances. I ended up remaking them. I painted them in shades of blue. Visually, I felt this helped a lot. You can't tell in this picture because it is black and white, but I wanted to mention it.

Credit: Audacity Theatre Lab

The trick it to make a good, useable set that serves your show. The scenery should not, however, draw attention away from your performance.

Though this looks like a lot of scenery, everything – minus furniture – packed down into a big duffle bag. When I travelled around to fringe festivals and venues away from my hometown, I would just use whatever tables and chairs I would find at the theatres. There is almost always a chair and little café table I can use laying around. I will touch on keeping your "touring kit" condensed and lightweight a little bit later.

You can definitely do a solo show with nothing on the stage at all, but I find things such as basic furniture pieces (chairs, side tables, coat racks, music stands, etc.) are handy as things to sit on, stand at, move around, climb on, lay across, crawl under or manipulate in some way. These things become anchor points to move toward or move away from. They become things to block around. They can also be easily customized with very few accessories.

I always carried a table cloth to drape over whatever table I found at a venue when I was touring *Chop*. This way I could keep the look of my show, more or less, consistent. The thing I wanted to avoid was what playwright and author Gary Garrison called the "we just pulled this out of our garage" look. Whatever set design you do include should look purposeful and coherent. It should look like it belongs in your show.

Blocking for Energy

Another thing that I try to keep in mind is something out of my own directing experiences. I try to keep in mind the level of energy in a scene. Some parts of the play are loud, some quiet. Some moments are really kinetic, some are meditative and still. Some are mysterious, some aggressive.

Pay attention to the pacing and the energy you want to put across to the audience. This helps determine movement around the stage and also helps to keep the show from being one note.

Keep Track of Your Progress

I have found it handy to keep a sort of project journal, especially for the first part of the creation process. I have been carrying a sketchbook with me for years. I still jot down ideas in that little journal to this day. I put down snippets of monologues and dialogue, doodle the look of characters, map out story structure, draw the stage picture and stream-of-conscious dump my thoughts and discoveries in the sketchbook.

Now that the world has become more digital, I don't always have my sketchbook on me. When I am out and about without my sketchbook, I type ideas into my phone. I use the Evernote app. I think any note-taking app would work. A colleague of mine uses Google Docs. I have a novelist friend who uses Notion. I like Evernote because I can cut-and-paste text out of it. Evernote also allows me to make tags and create "notebooks" for each project.

Sometimes, I'll collect all these disparate notes into a file on my computer. I'll scan or take a photo of the sketchbook notes and save them as PDFs. I'll move the notes from Evernote to Word docs. I use these to trace the progress of my project. Sometimes, I'll go back and look at an old idea and it will spark another idea.

The reason I think keeping all these little notes collected somehow, somewhere, is important is because it allows you to track the different iterations of your show. I am always surprised by how far a show develops over time. Those very first, initial ideas seem quaint by the time I get to the fourth or fifth draft and am up and performing the piece.

I have also, on occasion, borrowed a discarded idea from one project to use in another project. An abandoned bit of dialogue might be just the thing in another context. Or, more often, some idea that didn't fit indirectly prompts a new idea. If you haven't noticed yet, that notion of an idea building off of other ideas is sort of a theme of my overall creative process. A "project journal" is a great way to harvest those ideas.

The last really helpful aspect I have experienced keeping all my ideas, thoughts and drafts in one place is the ability to have a sort of dialogue with my own work. I often write down my reflections on the show I am putting together. I sort of write to myself like I am my own correspondent. While these contemplations don't always look like letters I might get in the mail, they could. Basically, I use the journal as a place to think stuff out. If I make discoveries or breakthroughs, I record them. If I get stuck on something, I record it. If I feel something is not working, I record it.

This approach might not work for you, but keeping a project journal has become part of my own process and I offer it as a suggestion to you.

Here are the take-aways: consider what scenery you need. What can improve the theatre experience? What is really essential? What can provide a set that can be interacted with? Try not to just stand there. And finally, try to use some sort of project journal to record cues, capture ideas and track progress.

CHAPTER 6 - PERFORMING YOUR SHOW

In this section we'll move on to the early stages of actually performing the show for audiences. The transition from rehearsing your show to performing it for audiences can sometimes be rocky. With adequate preparation and an open attitude, this transition will go a lot smoother.

Your First Show

Over the last few years, I have taken up camping and hiking, working my way towards an extended long-distance thru-hike. Thru-hiking can take weeks, even months, and cover hundreds, even thousands of miles. It can be a major endeavor.

There are two modes of thinking when it comes to training for a long hike. One approach is to simply use the first few weeks of the hike as a "break in" period. Walking ten to fifteen, or more, miles every day and camping out every night will force your body to adapt. This adaptation will be painful, especially at first, as your muscles and your mind adapt to the new routine.

The other approach is to hike short distances before the hike, gradually walking longer distances on a frequent schedule. This gives way to overnight trips, covering just a few miles, then multi-day trips covering more miles. Eventually, you work your way up to covering maybe 15 miles a day and are super comfortable being outside all day and night. This approach is more time-consuming because it is front-loaded and gradual. It is also considerably less painful than forcing your body to suddenly adapt. You will also probably enjoy the thru-hike more since you won't spend weeks in pain trying to get your act together.

Each approach has the same end result (if you don't give up) of making you into a thru-hiker, but one makes the period of preparation longer, gradually building up your hiking muscles and skill set with less pain. One method front-loads the preparation.

As a solo performer we want to mirror this longer approach.

Some performers use the first several productions to "break in" their show in front of paying audiences. They are okay with presenting a work-in-progress that is under-rehearsed and not ready. They figure the first few performances will let them get their "hiking-legs" under them.

This approach is disrespectful to the audience members that paid the ticket price to see the show. Your show must be ready for an audience or it should not be shown to an audience. Rehearse until it is ready.

Obviously, I am not talking about developmental opportunities such as staged readings or workshop productions. I'm also not referring to open mics, salons and such. These opportunities make it explicit to the audience that they are seeing and are part of the making process.

I'm referring directly to performers purposely putting up shows that they know are not quite ready.

In my opinion, this is half-ass and selfish. Audiences, especially paying audiences, are important and to purposely present an unfinished or not-quite-up-to-par show is not professional.

Maybe you are not quite sure if your show is ready. You can get through the whole thing without flubbing lines. You know conceptually, what happens in the story and are conscious of how it needs to be paced. But how do you know if it is ready enough to show to ticket buyers? The bar I set for myself is when I feel my show meets *spec*.

Meeting Spec

At some point, after you have rehearsed the play enough, you will reach what I call "spec." This is a term I borrowed from author and marketing guru Seth Godin. He used the phrase in regards to product development. According to Godin, when your product is clearly not defective in any way it becomes "good enough." Godin believes the product is then ready to go to market.

Meeting spec means your show is passable. It means it meets all relevant specifications. This is the point when your show can be presented, or exposed, to others.

It is important to note, this is not where the development of your show stops. It is not "done." The term "good enough" is a ridiculous concept in the performing arts. Things can always, ALWAYS be improved. Godin, of course, wasn't talking about an organic process like performing a show. He was referring to creating an app or selling a product of some kind. I use his term because it makes a good benchmark to delineate the end of rehearsals and the beginning of the performance stage of your show.

A Word About Deadlines

I don't know anyone who likes deadlines. In the performing arts, however, deadlines are inevitable. Once a show is announced to the public, the opening date and time will race closer until at the appointed hour you will find yourself on stage, ready or not, in front of an expectant audience.

Opening night is not the only deadline. If you are part of a festival you will find a series of deadlines to submit various information and materials. A blurb or description will need to be sent in months before you show up to perform. The same with production photos, promo videos and other materials. Missing these deadlines hurts the chances of ticket sales for your show, but also makes the job harder for festival organizers. On top of this, your reputation might suffer a bit if you continually miss deadlines.

Don't be that person.

I find deadlines stressful. The added pressure of working against the clock beyond the challenge of simply trying to creatively craft something into existence is head-ache inducing.

Deadlines, however, must be taken into account and respected. Make sure you give yourself enough time to create, rehearse and market (more on this in a future chapter) your piece leading up to a full production.

Some people might enjoy cramming and hustling to race deadlines, but I find, for me, there is too great a risk of shoddy work. If I get hurried, I tend to stress out and cut corners in the process. So, my advice is to stay ahead of deadlines. Falling behind just seems to make everything that is difficult even more so.

Pay Attention

I am not sure if other solo performers do this, but I actively make note of new discoveries, unforeseen problems that arise and surprising audience reactions through the beginning of the production process.

I find this exercise useful, especially for the first half dozen times or so I perform the show for audiences. I go back stage immediately after the show, take out a notebook and jot down any observations that stick out to me. It usually only takes a minute or two and I try to capture observations while it is fresh in my mind.

If I need to clear out of the space to make way for the next act, for example, if I am at a fringe festival with back to back programming, I will sit down somewhere to think over the show and make some notes. I do this as soon as I can after my show.

I am not sure where I picked up this little habit. Maybe this comes from the quick debriefs I used to do after long-form improv sets. The troupe would gather real quick after the show and mention what did and did not work. It was sort of equivalent to a notes session that a director might give after a rehearsal.

These notes, however, are from the perspective of me, the performer, within the eye of the storm, and, as I said, usually only takes a few minutes. I look over these notes before the next show so as to address changes that might need to be made. Sometimes it is talking with the board op about getting on a light cue quicker, or sometimes it is about telling myself not to rush a certain section or take a beat at a certain time to make a moment clearer.

Over time, the notes seem to get more granular. Little things stick out here and there that need tweaking. Honestly, as I continue to perform the show over time, I rarely keep looking back at these notes. However, I still find myself making them. Going through the motions of writing stuff down is usually enough to make it stick with me.

What do I do with these little notes? I usually jam them into my project journal. That way if I do need them, they are collected together to look to later.

I am not making a blanket recommendation of this to everyone, but I have tucked it into my own process and it seems to help me.

Remember, it is a Process

Even though you have now started performing your show for audiences, keep in mind, it is still a process. Your show should improve and deepen organically. You will, hopefully, get better at performing it. You may make discoveries as you go along that never would have occurred to you when you started rehearsing, let alone performing the piece for audiences.

Embrace that the piece will probably change. Do not try to "freeze" it in place. I am not talking about the lines and the blocking, hitting your marks and such. I am talking about getting the show to a certain level and then trying to keep right exactly there. It probably won't stay the exact same over time. Growth and change are natural and should be expected to some degree.

It should be mentioned, as well, that your piece will not be perfect. Ever. I have had better shows and worse, but I have never walked off stage and thought, "Sweet Zeus, that was a perfect performance…" In fact, I would argue that perfection is an unhelpful goal. You should be shooting for better, rather than perfect. What do I mean by *better*? I think better encompasses improved pacing, improved clarity, sharper comedic delivery, deeper emotional beats and a bunch of other idiosyncratic stronger choices and points of execution.

I do take into account the experience of the audience, because, of course, I want my performances to have impact and I want the audience enjoy the show. However, the response from the audience is not a reliable barometer for basing the value of your show on. Audiences vary and sometimes, as a collective, they are hard to read.

I have performed more than a few shows where the audience was really quiet and seemed really distant. Then, at the end of the show, I received a wonderful ovation. Or I have a bunch of audience members approach me with really positive feedback.

On the other hand, I have had the experience where I thought I was killing it on stage and the audience was with me every step of the way. Then by the end there is a lukewarm reception and the audience files out silently.

Over time, I have learned to judge my own performance from my own unique perspective. If I offer the gift of the show openly and I hit all my own cues, all my own emotional beats, and, also quite important, I have a good time presenting my show, then it is time well spent. I can only urge the audience in a certain direction. It would be utterly presumptuous of me to think I could somehow control how they receive what I present.

So, expect that the show will change, individual audiences are not great barometers and, regardless, you should strive to keep improving.

"But I have the show up on its feet. It's all set," you may declare. "It's fine as it is…"

Okay. That's great, but you deserve better and the audience definitely deserves better… every time.

I am reminded of two anecdotes. First, I think about a good friend of mine. He is a fantastic actor. He often, however, gets to a point where he is content to sort of "phone it in." When I press him on this, he mentions that the show or performance was "good enough." He points out that the audience enjoyed the show and, moreover, they don't have any point of comparison to a better version, so how would they know?

This guy is a good friend and, as I said, a really good actor, but this attitude irks me.

Fortunately, as he continues to mature as an actor, this attitude seems to be changing into one of constant improvement.

This second anecdote might help explain why this good-enough attitude irks me so..

The late, great stage director Sir Peter Brook once invited a friend of his to see the final performance of his show *Conference of the Birds*. During this run, the show had played continuously for nearly a year. The friend accompanied Brook back stage to wish well to the actors. Instead of simply giving everyone a hearty good show (which he did), Brook then pulled out a small notepad and begin to give very specific notes to the actors.

"Do remember to keep up the pace in the second scene."

That sort of thing.

The actors all nodded. Brook smiled, gave a small bow of gratitude to his troupe and then turned and left.

As Brook and his friend made their way to the front of house to take their seats to watch that evening's show, the friend turned and asked, in good-natured disbelief, about the notes.

"Haven't these same actors been performing this show eight times a week for the previous nine months?"

"Yes. Indeed, they have," answered Brook.

"And tonight is the last and final performance?"

"Yes, for now, it is."

"Then tell me, why are you still giving your actors notes on this last night?"

Brook, with a slightly bemused smile, but a completely serious tone turned to his friend and said, simply, "Why should this audience tonight be deprived a potential improvement?"

I love that. "Why should this audience tonight be deprived a potential improvement?"

So, remember, even when the show is set, it will change. Though it will never be perfect, it doesn't need to be. It just needs to be a little bit better, a bit more emotionally resonant, a bit more hilarious, a bit more dynamic for each new audience. It will, more than likely, be more fun to perform each time as well.

CHAPTER 7 – TOURING

For those new to touring, especially for performers who have only previously acted in their local theatres, what follows are a few tips to let you know what to expect and ways to save you some trouble. It will take a bit to get used to, but after a gig or two, you'll get the hang of it.

Touring just means instead of performing your show in one location for a long period of time, you take it on the road to perform for different audiences in other places. Tours can be to one far off city for a single long weekend, or you can go on the road for month, even years. I have some friends and colleagues who make their ways across Canada from east to west participating in a new fringe festival every few weeks all summer long.

You can perform in regional theatres, community theatres, pub theatres (in the UK), PACs or colleges and universities. Heck, I know some performers who set "living room" tours and did their shows in private residences for a few people at a time.

I am focusing mostly on fringe festivals as a good place for solo performers to start touring their shows. Fringes have a certain infrastructure in place to help newer performers as they get their shows on the road. There are small, newer fringes and there are large international fringes. The Edinburgh Fringe in Scotland and the Adelaide Fringe in Australia are big festivals that mix shows by emerging artists with established performers, even celebrities.

Many solo performers tour their work to as many venues as they can, so it's important to keep the show as technically simple as possible and not rely too much on special sound or lighting effects that may not be available on the road.

As discussed in chapter 5, I try to make sure whatever physical set pieces, props and costumes I need to take can fit in a normal size duffle bag. Sometimes, that isn't possible, of course, but that is my aim each time.

Touring Kit

I call the duffle bag where I keep all my stuff my "touring kit." It is usually a canvas duffle bag, sturdy with both regular handles as well as a shoulder strap. I write my name and contact info on a piece of gaff tape and affix it inside the bag.

Into this bag goes any props, set dressings (like the table cloth I mentioned in chapter 5 I used for *Chop*) and costume pieces that won't wrinkle too much. I also put in the bag an extra "clean" copy of my script, a flashdrive with back-up files and a few postcards in case I get to a venue and they have run out of the marketing materials I had previously dropped off or sent in.

There are several reasons I use a single duffle, if possible. Firstly, I place all this stuff in a single bag because I want everything in one place. I essentially want to be able to present the show from the stuff in that bag. Often, there will be a secure place where you can leave your show stuff backstage at the venue you are performing in. There will be a taped-off area backstage or in a dressing room. This, however, is not always the case.

With everything contained in a single bag, you keep your stuff out of the way of other acts that might be sharing that venue with you. Unfortunately, I have witnessed fellow performers, solo and otherwise, in the past sprawl their materials all over the place backstage. Not only is this disorganized and a good recipe for losing things, but your stuff gets in the way of others.

Maybe it is these instances that have ruined it for everyone else at certain venues.

Every so often, I participate in a festival where they insist that the performer "load-out" everything after each show. Load-put just means you have to take everything with you that you might have brought in. You basically have to completely strike your show after each performance. The festival or venue manager will offer vague or arbitrary explanations for this policy. However, this is hugely inconvenient, especially for the solo performer. It means you, alone, will have to break-down and repack ALL of your show stuff after each show and then lug it around with you.

If you are meeting friends after a show and heading out to dinner or drinks, or seeing another show after your own, then you have to haul your show stuff around with you.

This was the case one year when I took a show to a fringe festival in New York. I was in a third floor theatre space in a small theatre in Greenwich Village. The Venue Manager, a surly volunteer with very little theatre experience, informed me and the other acts in the space that we had to take everything with us after each of our shows. There was obviously room to leave things in the backstage area for the four or five shows sharing the space. When I explained the problem with this, she cited a small-print line in the festival handbook. She was a very by-the-book sort of person. At the time, I had my stuff in a giant cargo bag on wheels.

I remember lugging that thing on and off the subway, into bars, trying to stow it under restaurant booths and toting it into other venues to see other people's shows. I was staying in the Park Slope area of Brooklyn at a friend's place and taking the bag directly back after each show would have meant pretty much staying in Brooklyn for the rest of the day. I was also pretty much on foot the whole time. Taxis were expensive and this was before the days of Uber and Lyft.

Moreover, I saw most of the other shows that shared my venue, and none had elaborate, fragile or voluminous scenery.

If you participate in a festival or perform at a venue, particularly as a solo performer, and are made to load-out after each and every show, make sure you send feedback to the festival organizers after the experience to let them know this practice was not cool.

This is one reason I aim for a single duffle bag, at most. Better it, than various trunks and crates that need a team of porters to transport. In fact, after that New York show so many years ago, I decided I wouldn't let some small, but hugely inconvenient rule like loading-out become a detriment to my performing experience in the future. Now my touring kit consists of one duffle bag.

Of course, if festivals and venues do away completely, as a matter of course, with removing all show materials after every single performance, then a single bag approach to touring might not be such a big deal.

Sometimes, I don't even need the duffle bag. It is often amazing how far one can get with a table cloth, hat and one well-chosen prop.

Back Up Drive

Besides a paper print-out of my script, as a back-up tech script (left "blank" so a Board Op can write in the cues as needed), I also carry a small thumbdrive with a copy of the script as a Word doc and as a PDF on it.

In fact, I have all the digital materials for my show backed up on this thumbdrive. It has on it copies of:

- My Electronic Press Kit
- PDF and JPEG of my poster image (in case I need to print off more while on the road)
- PDF and JPEG of my postcard image (in case something happens to the postcards I brought and I need to print them off on cardstock in an emergency).
- A file with all of my travel info (flight itinerary or car rental info, hotel address or billet contact).
- A file with contact info for the festival or venue I am traveling to.
- Schedule of my tech and shows.
- Any other information I think it would be beneficial to have on hand.

This little back-up thumbdrive has saved me several times in the past. I was at one festival years ago and was invited to go on the radio and be interviewed. About two hours before I was due to go on the air, live, the producer of the radio show contacted me and asked for a blurb of the show, a short bio and any quotes from good reviews they could use to introduce me. I had all that info on my thumbdrive and emailed it over within ten minutes. Having it at the ready meant I didn't have to compile it on the road. I got to the interview a few minutes early, of course, and the producer pulled me aside and thanked me for being so "fast and professional." The little interview segment went great.

Observe Others

I have learned a great deal about touring my shows by both talking with and observing how my colleagues handle touring. You can think of touring as a set of overlapping segments. One segment is finding and submitting to a festival or venue. I will touch on that in a bit. Another segment of touring is the actual travel to the place where you will be performing. Another segment is setting up a place to stay while in that city performing. Another segment is how you communicate with festival or venue staff, how you go through tech. Another is how you market your show both before and during the run of your show. Another segment is getting the most out of your experience as both a performer and as a spectator/supporter of other people's shows.

Other performers who have been touring awhile have probably come up with little systems for themselves filled with tips and tricks about how they handle things. For instance, my friend Grant Knutson covers hundreds and hundreds of miles each year in his car visiting fringes all over North America. He told me that a great way to stock up on simple supplies when getting to a new town was to find the local Dollar Store. You know, one of those stores that sells everything either for a dollar or just really cheap. This was great advice for replacing toiletries, batteries, getting bottles of water and simple snacks and so on.

Another colleague berated me online once when I admitted that I bought the packaging tape I would tape up my posters with at a common drug store. He was adamant that I needed to get the best tape available, with a sturdy tape dispenser. He had experienced cheap tape not sticking and getting tangled as he tried to tape up posters. I adopted his advice and you know what? Putting up posters got quicker and easier simply by investing in higher quality tape and one of those dispensers with a handle.

So, I'd like to offer a few helpful tips on some of the segments that make up touring with your solo show that maybe don't get covered a lot.

Factor in the Vagaries of Travel

If you perform your show out of town, then you will need to decide how to get there. Early on, I used up a lot of frequent flyer miles I had saved getting to far off cities to perform in festivals. If I had to supply my own tech person, I sometimes drove and split the cost of gas with that person. Flying is kind of a hassle, but quicker. Driving is sometimes (but not always) cheaper, but takes longer. I have also taken buses and trains in the past. And even a ferry when needing to cross a strait.

However you decide to get to wherever you are going, make sure you factor in the unpredictability of travel and transportation. If your tech time is at 5:00 pm on a Wednesday, then maybe you should book an earlier flight than the one that is scheduled to land in your destination city at 4:00 pm. That is cutting it too close.

Same goes for leaving after the final show in a run. If your last show ends on a Sunday at 8:00 pm and you book a flight for 9:30 pm, you are cutting things very, very close.

I always allow a bit of a cushion for the inevitable hold-ups that pop up. You can almost always expect some unexpected thing to cause problems. You'll get lost finding the venue the first time. Your flight will be delayed (or worse, cancelled. That has happened to me enough to make it a consideration). Parking is always an issue. You don't factor in saying goodbyes or rush hour traffic or one hundred and one other little things that can put you behind schedule.

The take away here is to give yourself some cushion when traveling. Things never seem to go as smoothly as I plan for them to and I don't think that is just me. I think this sense of hiccups happening while traveling happens to everyone. Certainly solo performers.

Where to Stay

One of the challenging parts of touring is figuring out where to stay. My first choice is to stay with someone I know, but that is not always an option, particularly if I don't know anyone in the city I might be traveling to. Hotels can be expensive, especially if you need to be in a place more than a few nights. Fortunately, if you participate in theatre festivals, often they will help performers find accommodations.

Billeting is a term you will encounter if you tour to fringe festivals. The festival will set up a local "host" who has a space, guest room or even a vacant couch or air mattress that can be thrown down in the living room. The out-of-town performer is provided with a place to stay for free. Usually the festival will offer the host free or heavily discounted admission to any and all shows at that year's fringe. Win, win, right? Well, kind of.

Not all billets are created equal. The privacy of a guest room after a long trip and the stress of performing and marketing your show is far different than sleeping in someone's living room with zero privacy. Some hosts are more hospitable than others. And some billets are farther away from the venues than others.

A billet is like a free AirBnB with a certain degree of hassle-risk. If you are looking to save money and don't mind an added element of adventure, give billeting a try.

The one thing I learned rather early is to contact your billet hosts and introduce yourself as soon as you can. Ask them to take a photo of the actual space where you will be staying and to send it to you. This one tip has saved me tons of head-aches over the years. I know what to expect if I can physically see the space. For instance, if I am going to be on the floor, then I am sure to pack my own inflatable air mattress (the one I use for camping), so I am sure to get a good night's sleep.

Compile a short list of things you are curious about into a single email for your hosts to answer before you arrive. For example, if there is no internet access at the billet I want to know before I arrive. If there is public transport not far from the host's place, I want to know about it.

Budgeting for Touring

Touring your show probably will not make you rich. Or, I should say, I do not personally know anyone who has gotten wealthy from traveling around presenting solo shows. That said, it is not automatic that you will lose money touring. You do get anywhere from 60% to 100% of ticket sales at most fringe fests and regular theatre engagements. Sometimes, for non-fringe engagements you'll need to negotiate that percentage. The more people who pay the admission price to see your show, the more you make. That is not the only way to make a little profit from solo performing. Here are a few ways to come out ahead financially, even if just slightly.

First, find ways to lower your overhead. I will touch on this more in Chapter 10. Technically, it shouldn't cost you a fortune to mount a solo performance. Most one-person shows, by their nature, are not super elaborate. Costs that are automatic for traditional theatre productions, like paying to rent rehearsal space are more flexible for the solo performer. I rehearse most of my shows in my office or living room. I do my own designing, promoting and web design. Since my first show, I have directed myself in my solo shows. I book my own travel, I answer my own emails and I usually use whatever technicians are included in a festival venue or on staff at a theatre. All of this takes a lot of time and energy to set up, but not money.

If you can do something yourself, do it. I am a big advocate for the performer taking full responsibility for his or her show. Learning the basics of graphic design, marketing and administration (which is a fancy word for scheduling and communication) means you do not need to pay others to do stuff for you. These all have learning curves, of course, but if you stick with solo performance, it is probably beneficial to pick up these adjacent skill sets as you go along.

Lowering your overhead means not getting extravagant with physical properties, scenery and costumes. It means traveling cheaply and taking advantage of things like billeting.

For instance, I will make postcards for a show and leave half of the space on the back blank. I will print off mailing label stickers with the specific information for specific engagements. At the end of an engagement, I will gather up whatever postcards didn't get handed out and use them again, just putting a new sticker with new info on them for the next engagement. As long as I am diligent about going back to recollect whatever postcards were not taken at the end of a festival I can stretch an initial order of several hundred postcards out over several fringe fests before I need to re-order.

Travel is often one of the financially costlier parts of touring. There are a lot of ways to save money when traveling. I maintain frequent flyer miles for air travel and hotel points in case I don't have a billet where I am going. I am not above riding a bus if I have the time and am not traveling more than half a day on the road. I use public transport or Lyft/Uber when I get to destinations where I will perform. Or I borrow a bicycle from someone. Occasionally, I unlock those little rental scooters to get around. Or ask for rides. Or walk.

Traveling on a budget is often harder than flying in luxury or driving one's own car places, but it is very doable. There are plenty of resources online and elsewhere for ways to "hack" travel. In any case, saving money on travel expenses is a good way to lower overhead costs of touring.

So, keep your overhead low and diversify what you can offer up and beyond just the show itself. Of course, ideally, you will profit the most from getting a lot of people to see your shows and then sell-out each and every performance (he says, tongue firmly in cheek). For this to happen you are going to need to market your show well. That is what the next chapter will cover.

CHAPTER 8 – MARKETING PART 1

First, a little intro of sorts...

Let me be clear up front, I am not a marketing professional. Everything I am about to lay out is from my own experience, observation and research. Marketing is one of the parts of solo performing I was most ill-at-ease with when starting out. Since it was the most mysterious and labyrinthine, I have endeavored to be pretty thorough in this section and to fill it to the brim with information. Though I present a bunch of info below, I admit, I do not always follow all of my own advice.

Not all performance opportunities are the same. Marketing a run of a show at a specific venue on its own is different than participating in a fringe festival. And then, fringe festivals vary greatly, too. So, take what you can from the info below, but don't feel it is the only way to do things. In fact, I'm sure I am probably leaving some stuff out that I will forget about until after I see this book come out and then I will kick myself for not including it.

I am working from the stance that you, the reader, has little to no experience marketing a one-person show. You are probably curious about how to get started and, like myself (until fairly recently), may have a high degree of resistance to the mere mention of the word.

When I was starting out and looking for advice on how to market a one-person show, I kept reading vague recommendations like "Spread the word" or "Get the word out." I remember thinking, "Well yeah, of course. That sounds great. But how exactly do I do that?"

Because this part of solo performance is probably the most foreign to most performers (it certainly was for me), I'm splitting the discussion on marketing into two parts. This first part will be about setting up a platform with all the materials you'll need to make your marketing easier across the board. In another section I will go over how to market "on the ground," such as at a fringe festival or just before your show goes up at a theatre venue.

So, this chapter is for those who don't know quite where to start. For those with a good amount of experience already, maybe this section of the book will offer some refreshers or even spark a few new ideas. Maybe it will just offer a good laugh.

I will cover what marketing is, why marketing is so important for the individual solo performer, how to build a foundation in order to make the task easier and, lastly, encourage a sturdy DIY approach that will, hopefully, put more butts in seats for the show you have worked so hard to create.

What do you mean "Marketing?"

The definition of marketing is: the action or business of promoting and selling products or services. The word marketing, particularly in the world of live performing arts, has garnered some negative connotations in recent times. It can be considered crass or schmaltzy, aggressive or overbearing.

On the other hand, I have read marketing described in altruistic terms, too. In his book *Your First 1000 Copies*, book marketing expert Tim Grahl describes marketing as "first and foremost about helping people." Type marketing into a search on the internet and words like "connection" and "community" sometimes pop up, especially by marketing "gurus" who want to, surprise, sell you on the concept of marketing (and the services they provide in that department).

I do not quite subscribe to the theory that marketing (and its darker shadow *promotion*) builds community in and of itself. It doesn't "create value" on its own. And it is only of service in so far as it helps inform would-be audience members about a theatre experience. That theatre experience, not the message about the experience, might actually add value to their lives.

For our purposes, I am going to keep it super simple. Marketing, here, just means the ways one gets the word out about the show you are performing. After all, people need to know about what you are doing before they can check out what you are doing.

Doing It Yourself

Most solo performers I know, myself included, do their own marketing. Or, at least, they haphazardly try to do their own marketing.

Rare is the emerging solo performer who can afford to hire a marketing team to help promote his or her show. It is not unheard of for really big festivals like the Edinburgh, Adelaide or maybe the New York International Fringe for a performer to hire help. That approach, on a regular basis, can prove to be very expensive. Because of the expense, there is little chance of recouping those costs. If someone can afford a marketing team, many times those performers have usually spent many years and massive energy becoming recognized enough to work at a high enough level to warrant a marketing team. This is a big generalization, but people with marketing teams are often aiming to turn the thousands of fans they already have into tens of thousands of fans.

If you can afford a marketing or PR person or firm, and there is a chance at making enough profit to make that decision worthwhile, by all means, do it. Not only will it teach you a lot, but from what I can observe, having professional help really can translate to putting more butts in seats.

In this book, I am working from the assumption that you do not yet garner "name recognition" in the cities, venues and festivals you will be taking your show to and that you will be handling the marketing of your show yourself.

"But wait," you might say, "doesn't the festival or venue handle the marketing for me?"

Yes and no. A fringe festival, solo fest, PAC or a theatre company will do some marketing. They will promote you on their website and maybe send some emails out to their lists about your show. They may even line up some interviews or profiles for you with local press or arts bloggers.

But...

A festival's main focus is to market the festival as a whole. There will probably be no special regard for your individual show. Same goes for theatre companies. Theatres customarily do multiple productions every season. They concentrate on selling their subscribers on a whole package of shows, of which your show is only one part. Venues like performing arts centers are the same. They load up on programming to offer to their subscribers and your show is just one of many.

You should be the one to step up and champion your show. Organizers of festivals and producers at theatres not only appreciate when solo performers take an active role in marketing their own shows, to some degree it is expected nowadays. This is especially true if you are attending a small festival.

Smaller theatre festivals are often understaffed and the organizers, bless their little hearts, are just trying to keep all the balls in the air to sustain and grow their festival. These folks don't have the time, money, staff, resources or incentive to concentrate on promoting specifically your show.

A performer who shows up and does nothing to help promote his or her own work is dead weight. This is often perceived by the festival organizer in a negative light. The performer comes off like he or she is doing the festival a favor by just, you know, showing up. The result is a no-win situation for everyone.

The bottom line is that if potential audiences don't know about your show, you can be sure they won't come out to see it. And your duty is to do everything in your power to make sure that potential audiences do know about your show.

Performers who don't do anything (or very little) to market their shows often face crushingly small audiences. This is embarrassing for everyone involved. You created and prepared your show, putting in large amounts of hard work and care as well as time and energy, and then you traveled to a far off festival or venue at no small expense. Then you walk out on stage, the lights come up and you see only five people in the audience. This knowledge comes in those first few moments as you begin to perform and by that time, when you realize you could/should have done so much more to get the word out, it is too late to do anything about it. It can be demoralizing.

I have performed for my share of small audiences. In fact, years ago at a now-defunct festival in Phoenix, Arizona, I performed a solo show for one audience member. It was very conversational. Don't get me wrong, I prefer decent-to-large sized crowds. However, I am not disturbed when I have the odd super-small audience.

I don't see solo performers talk about their audience sizes that often (unless it is to grumble about low attendance), but I have observed that I get about what others at my level seem to get, give or take. On average, I usually perform for between 10 and 50 audience members at a time these days. This usually translates to an average of 40 – 80% of the house, depending on the size of the venue. Most of the time, I am performing solo shows in smaller theatres. Occasionally, I will sell-out, sometimes I do shows still for a small handful of audience members. Maybe someday, I'll fill stadiums, but, for now, I am fine with a few dozen folks. The nice thing about solo work is that usually it lends itself to an intimate presentation.

Side note here: Appreciate whatever audience you get. Don't be that performer who gets all aloof and snooty when audiences are low. Whoever makes it out to see your show is there for you. I have observed performers who turn in a subpar performance for small audiences. Their performance isn't bad, per se, but they don't seem to put as much effort in. The rationalization is a small audience just isn't worth the effort. Avoid being this jerk. Have gratitude for whoever shows up and give them a performance to remember.

However, you do need some people in the audience. Performing does not exist in a vacuum. This is especially true if you are doing comedy.

For comedy there is an unofficial magic number of the minimal amount you need in order to get a whole room laughing. For the life of me, I cannot remember what that number is. Maybe it is ten. I can't remember who told me about it or where it was that I read it. I thought it was in *Born Standing Up*, a fantastic book by Steve Martin about his career as a stand-up comedian. But when I sat down to write this, I couldn't find that observation in his book anywhere.

Martin does, however, point out that the audience must be in darkness. People do not feel as free to laugh when the house lights are up. Anyway, the take away is, laughter is contagious. You need at least enough audience members that those in the house don't feel insecure about openly laughing at and engaging with your performance.

Shows that are not marketed enough, with small audiences, are difficult for all involved. You, as a performer, feel let down. The tech crew feels sorry for you. The festival organizers are both apologetic to you and sorry for you at the same time.

What Are You Selling?

Live performance is ephemeral. That is both the glory and curse of it. When it comes to marketing your show, your goal is to rally a group of human beings to be in a certain place at a certain time in order to experience your show. And a live production has to be experienced in real time. This is a tall order in the contemporary world of on-demand/ streaming content.

To get people to the show, you need to be clear about what it is you are selling them on. I have found there are three areas you can focus on in that regard. You can try to sell yourself as the performer, you can try to sell the performance itself, or you can try to sell some combination of both.

Comedians, for instance, do not promote the content of their shows. They don't market this great stand-up set about becoming a new dad, their bits about marriage or living the life of a touring comic. Instead they market themselves. Come see this person, because this person is super funny. Bands do the same thing. Come see this band, you'll like their music. They don't promote a show saying, come see this gig where we play songs about heartbreak.

Filmmakers on the other hand, market the content of their films. There is an emphasis on story or action or romance. Novelists work in a similar fashion. They promote a particular story in a particular genre such as thrillers or fantasy or sci-fi.

Occasionally, you'll see an artist who is as well-known as the work they do. These are the Beyonces, the Quentin Tarantinos, the Neil Gaimans or Stephen Kings. Stephen King, the writer, is as known as much as the work he creates.

I think it is possible, even if you are not super well-known, to market some combination of yourself as an artist as well as the show you are doing. This is especially true if you are returning to a venue you have been to before or you have built up a small body of work people might know you from.

Titles Are Part of the Content

You should probably start thinking about the marketing of your show as early as the development process. For instance, the title should be something good and catchy. You don't want the title to be too generic, but you also don't want it to be confusing. If it is hard to pronounce or sort of cryptic then the title might make your show more challenging to market.

My friend Grant Knutson has been a consultant for fringe performers for a decade and half. He often repeats a continual interaction he has with touring fringe performers. Here's Grant:

> "A lot of performers will say, 'The title will make sense once the audience sees the show.' And I tell them that first you need those people to actually come in and see your show. The show is not your hook. The marketing is your hook. You want your poster image, flyers, blurbs, and so on - yeah, even the title of your show – to work for you, not against you. Is it confusing? Clever? Will is stand out? Don't make your marketing cryptic or mysterious or it will remain a mystery because people won't be drawn in to see it."

I consider myself pretty experienced at this point about solo performance, but even I make blunders from time to time. I titled one of my more recent shows *The Beast of Hyperborea*. I didn't think it was hard to spell or say, but as soon as I began trying to get the word out for the first festival I sent it to, I realized it had a slightly confusing quality to it. The word "Hyberborea," especially, was something that people looked past. It wasn't a hard word, but because it was unfamiliar, it *looked* like a hard word. People just kind of shut off their brains and the title of the show never caught on.

You ever meet someone with an unusual name? Either it is pronounced in a unique way or it is spelled funky. Or maybe you are not from the culture where that name is more common. The person may say it a few times to you, but because it is unfamiliar, you are always second guessing yourself when you say the name out loud. Or worse, you don't even remember the name because it originally demanded too much mental effort and now it is too late to ask them to say their name again for you. You go through each interaction with them trying not to get in a situation where you have to say that person's name out loud.

Try to make the title easy to read, but striking enough to stand out. It will help in your marketing efforts.

Build Your Own Skills!

I have met a fair amount of solo performers in the time I have been following and involved in this stuff. I have heard performers exclaim with a perverse sense of pride "I just don't know how to do it, so I sort of ignore marketing, hold my breath and hope for the best."

I have also heard more than a little complaining about marketing. The refrain goes something like this:"I made the show. Isn't that enough? I wish someone else would just sell it for me…" or "But marketing is so hard... I hate it!" Or "I just don't like to talk about myself (or my show) like that. I don't enjoy selling myself..." This last camp is where I use to set up my own tent.

I used to be one of these people who hated the very idea of marketing. I was content just to make things and release those things silently into the world and then go on to make more things. The result was that nothing I made had much of an impact. It took me an embarrassingly long time to realize I needed to be the main champion of my own work.

Nowadays, when I hear performers complaining about marketing I always feel a little sad for these folks. They are putting themselves in a position of victimhood. They are essentially saying they *can't be bothered* to market their own work. They feel overwhelmed about it and so don't even try.

I am a lot more forgiving of performers who try to market themselves and their work, even if they aren't super-good at it yet. They don't just throw up their hands and say, "Nothing to be done," but instead dig in. They will not be great at first, no one is, but they will get better and better. Experience and attention will naturally make them better with time.

I feel, even today, I am kind of playing catch-up after years of trying to ignore the whole marketing aspect of things. I am gradually getting better at it as I learn and apply more marketing to each show I do.

So, first take-away: Marketing is a learned skill, you know, like everything else. Just because you don't know how to do it well now doesn't mean you can't get better over time.

Second, and perhaps more important, marketing is mandatory. I will touch on this a bit later, but take this in: marketing your show is not really *optional*. Sticking your head in the ground because you don't want to deal with it will not change that fact. Theatre is a medium that needs an audience. That potential audience will definitely not show up at a show that they don't even know is happening. If a tree falls in the woods and no one is around to hear it and all that.

Baring these two points in mind, that marketing can be learned and that it is not optional, where to begin...

You Need a Platform

One of the more challenging aspects of marketing that took me a while to get a handle on was generating the materials I would need for marketing and keeping those things organized. After writing a press release over again, from scratch, a few times, I learned that I should just save a template of it. After trying to come up with a fresh blurb describing my show each time I applied to a festival, I eventually realized that I just needed to write out a good one and then cut-and-paste it as needed. It just had to be easily accessible somewhere. I sort of stumbled onto what I now call a marketing platform.

So, before we get to the actual things one does to market one's show, let's get a good foundation under us to make everything else easier down the road.

I have good news and bad news. Bad news first. The bad news is that the bulk of the work will come at the beginning, setting things up. There are more than a few materials you will need to put together to have on tap as you start the process of marketing your show. The good news is that you once you have all your materials together, you do not have to reinvent the wheel every time you take your show to a different venue or festival.

So, in this section I am going to discuss the materials you'll need to create, gather and so on. I will also focus on the container to put these basic things in. This container is what I am calling a *marketing platform*.

This is not a new idea. Artists in other fields have different versions of, essentially, the same thing. Visual artists post their portfolios on online websites. Filmmakers post samples of their work online and links to relevant interviews and press profiles. I am particularly inspired by what indie authors have been doing the last several years... something called an author platform.

Basically a marketing platform is exactly what it sounds like. I'm talking about a metaphorical elevated surface from which you can communicate information and where people can gather to "listen" to you. It is a presentation of you and your show that serves as a point of accessible connection between you and your audiences (or potential audiences). It serves as your marketing HQ. You can think of it as a virtual shelf for storing all of your marketing materials. Ideally, your marketing platform also serves to attract media, loyal followers who will spread the word about you and, most importantly, potential ticket buyers.

A platform is predominantly about communication and accessibility. As you may have guessed, a marketing platform exists pretty much online these days.

Technology has changed some fundamental ways we communicate. Pretty much everything is now digital. With this change, perceptions about what is essential to promote your show and how that message gets out have changed. For instance, what used to be an added bonus about a decade ago, like a good promo video, are now necessary to really get the word out about your show. It is super beneficial for you to learn to harness new enabling tools on the web as they arise and to build a flexible, but sturdy platform.

Also, a marketing platform offers a degree of communication that goes beyond just the connection the solo performer has directly with the audience during his or her show. With a strong presence online in the form of a website, email list, strategic social media and so on, connection with your audience can be an ongoing thing. You can build anticipation leading up to your show and it is a great way to get feedback and follow up after you've left the theatre and the actual physical proximity of your audience.

What's in a Marketing Platform?

To start out, I believe a solo performer needs three things in order to build a great foundation from which you can successfully start marketing your show:

- A website
- A press kit
- An email list

Let's take a look at each of these three components and how they function together.

A Website

This is your primary home base. This is where you send folks who are interested in finding out about your work.

In the past, creating a website meant knowing how to code. If you didn't know html, then you had to hire someone to make a website for you and also depend on that person to update it for you. Thankfully, things are much easier nowadays.

There are plenty of drag-and-drop options such as Wordpress, Wix, Weebly and so on (I never noticed before how many of these companies start with W). It is easier than ever to create a good-looking and functional website on your own. If it seems daunting, don't worry. A brief online tutorial will have you most of the way there in very little time. And the emphasis here is YOU. You, making a website yourself, with instant control of when and how it is updated is essential.

There are plenty of places online to find out what makes a compelling, well-designed website. I am not going to go into all of the best practices for creating a website here. I can say, designing a good website with the tools and resources available nowadays is not difficult. Here are a few things to definitely include on your site, content-wise:

- good images of you performing your show
- a concise blurb about what your show is about

- all the info of where and when your show is happening next, including location, address, dates, times, ticket info, etc.
- biographical information about you
- links to social media pages

You may also want to consider posting a promo (short for "promotional") video. I'll discuss that when we get to the Press Kit section. Also, you may also consider putting audience testimonials, links to good press and reviews and even study guides on your website.

Remember, people will seek out your website because they want information about you and your show, so make the site easy to navigate and that it has the information about the show prominent and readable.

Also, there are a few basic rules of etiquette when it comes to making websites you may want to keep in mind. Make sure everything is spelled correctly and that any and all links work. Also, have some sort of Contact page. You may only put your email address on it, but it is a good way to let press know where they can get a hold of you. It is also a good way to potentially get feedback from audiences who saw your show.

The most useful aspect of a website, besides the fact that you control the look and messaging, is that it can be a repository for information into the future. For instance, on my own personal "home base" website, I keep a list of every gig I have done dating back to

1994. It is always there for others to see, but more importantly, it is there for me to reference. I also have links to the press I've received, from profiles to reviews to my own contributions to various media outlets on a whole variety of topics. Maybe you have news you need to post somewhere. If you gather information about yourself and your show and you wonder, "Where do I put this stuff?" the answer is invariably to put it on your website.

Perhaps you are saying to yourself, "I have a Facebook page. Isn't that enough?" Or, "I have Twitter and Instagram and TikTok and a Tumblr. I don't need a website."

I say, "No. You still need a website."

A website is your own turf. It is yours. No matter what Facebook does to its algorithms or what changes when Instagram is sold to some other company or how many characters Twitter allows, your website is in your control. It is an evergreen place on the internet for you to call home and collect your information. I think of my personal website as my online portfolio. Again, it is a repository. And it is essentially ground zero for marketing purposes.

[Note: Google customized searches beginning in December 2009. Since then, no two people ever really see the internet the same way. Everything online runs on algorithms nowadays. Social media can be helpful for marketing purposes, but should not be solely relied on. Your posts may not be seen by as many people as you think.]

A Word About Your Domain Name

A domain name refers to your website address. This is what users type in a browser's search bar to directly access your website. Your domain name, also called a URL, is nothing more than the address of a given unique resource on the Web. URL means Uniform Resource Locator. It usually shows up as:

http://www.nameofyoursite.com or something like that.

A lot of website builder sites offer free domains, but you have to have their name as part of the URL. For instance, if you use the free version of Wordpress the URL will read something like:

http://www.nameofyoursite.wordpess.com

I do not mind this when I am simply creating a website for a specific show. If you put the title of your show prominently on the home page of your site and in the metadata, most search engines will find it easy enough.

You can always buy a domain name later and upgrade your website URL if you need to. I would strongly consider this if I were taking a particular show to a big festival or doing an off-Broadway run and needed it to look like it was part of a big professional outfit. However, for most smaller fringes and just general use, I stick with the free options.

For instance, for my show *Robert's Eternal Goldfish*, I created a "show" site. The URL is:

https://dribblefunk.wixsite.com/robseternalgoldfish

It looks cumbersome and overly long, doesn't it? However, if you type the title of the show "Robert's Eternal Goldfish" into a search engine, that site comes up among the first two or three search results.

I do have what I call a "home base" website. The domain is just my name:

http://www.BradMcEntire.com

I also have a custom URL for my playwriting endeavors [www.BradMcEntirePlays.com]. You might be asking why I have separate show websites if I have sites already that are dedicated to my creative work. I do this because I frequently have a lot of irons in the fire. I don't just do one thing creatively. Solo performance is just one of the many artistic pursuits I have. My home website encompasses a lot more than just my solo shows. The downside of this comes when I want to really focus on one of those shows. I found, over time, I needed a distinct place to send folks that just centered on a particular show and not on me as an all-over-the-place creative type.

If you are putting a website together for yourself as a performer, then I recommend you register your own URL. Usually, the advice is to have your name in the domain. As a long term investment it is worth the money paid to register your own domain name. It may help with search results when people want to find you on the internet. It definitely looks more professional. There are a lot of places to register a unique domain name online. I use Register.com, but in the past have used GoDaddy and others.

The decision of whether to make a show-specific site or a sort of all-encompassing website for yourself as a performer is, of course, up to you. Either way, I strongly advise you create for yourself some sort of website for your solo show projects.

The Electronic Press Kit (EPK)

A press kit is one of the important things that I don't see enough solo performers utilizing. A good press kit can be of great use to the performer as well as for, you know, the press. It can be a great way for a solo performer to introduce what he or she does. It can be a great way to sum up who you are, what you are about and what your show is about. And it does so in a tidy little press/media-friendly package.

In this section I want to explore what is in a standard contemporary electronic press kit, how press kits have changed over the last several years and how a press kit can be utilized.

First, what is a press kit? Traditionally, a press kit was a packet of photos and information given out to press and media folks that offered all kinds of stuff about your show. Up until about two decades ago, a press kit literally had large format, clear photos (with accompanying rights to further print these photos), a biographical write-up about the performer, a summation about the project/show and a listing of contact information for reviewers, critics and other journalists to use in order to follow-up. It came in a well-organized folder.

Eventually, this gave way to placing all the information on a CD, then eventually a flashdrive, and now almost all "press kits" are done online, via a website. These contemporary press kits are often referred to as EPKs, or Electronic Press Kits, since everything is digitalized. Sometimes this stuff is not referred to at all by name (I have heard very few solo performers actually use the phrase Electronic Press Kit), but the contents of an EPK are called for all the time.

Next, what would you need in a press kit? If you are doing good and interesting work at some point you are going to be featured on someone's blog, podcast, YouTube channel or maybe in some form of traditional media (alt weekly, newspaper, radio). Interviewers, bloggers and podcasters - in fact, all press/media people - are pretty busy folks. Why not make their lives a little easier? An organized, professional press kit will make them look good by keeping them on deadline and keeping them accurate and it will help them make you look good. It will also help them help you promote your show to their readers/viewers/listeners. Best of all, it will help you control your own personal branding.

Here are the elements that make up a good press kit for a given show...

Press Kit Checklist:

☐ **Press release**

A press release should have a few things...

- clear and engaging headline

- Specific info about your show like dates, times, location (like you might put on an invitation).
- quickly tells the reader what they need to know about your show (i.e lead with story about the show, not you or your "brand"... unless you are famous and that is the draw).
- a bit of context (world premiere? award-winning show? Based on an actual event? Taps into the zeitgeist in some way?)
- book end the release with more, and more complete, info about your upcoming show

Remember, your press release needs to be informative, but not dry. You're still selling your show. Ask yourself, why it is newsworthy?

"Why is it newsworthy?" is really the essential question. This is another way of asking "why should anyone come see your show?" Answering this in a concise way is the starting point for not just a good press release, but for marketing your show in general.

Newsworthy means it has a potential impact. It could be relevant and timely, emotionally raw, uproariously hilarious, thrilling, satirical, or a thousand other things. Emphasize why someone might be drawn to your show.

Here's an example from one of my recent solo shows. I am lifting this paragraph right out of the middle of one of my press releases:

> *The Beast of Hyperborea* is an astonishing tale told by a reluctant eye-witness. Joseph Reade, "an accountant by trade" finds himself drawn into an amazing adventure with an eccentric group of brave explorers who set off in search of a mythical creature on an undiscovered island. The account is presented in the tradition of Victorian adventure fiction (think Jules Verne, H. Rider Haggard, H.G. Wells and Arthur Conan Doyle).

Use natural language in a storytelling manner and avoid jargon. Be sure to read it back over to spell-check your work and to catch any weird grammar issues.

There are a lot of resources for how to put together good press releases online. You might even reach out to a local theatre or performing arts group and ask them to email you a copy of one of their press releases from a current show. That way you can have a look at how they do it.

I will be honest… I made a press release years ago and have just switched out the info over and over again on a show by show basis. Once you have sort of a template, you really don't need to reinvent the wheel from scratch each time.

☐ **At *least* four (4) hi-res images***

- Two (2), at minimum, "in performance" photos. (At least one horizontal and one vertical. These should be taken close enough to see your face, should show you in action and should be clear and engaging. It can also help to have different ones that have you are facing in different directions in the photos.)
- Your show poster or graphic
- A good headshot

All these photos should have proper accreditation in the name of the photo, specifically in the actual metadata.

Customarily, you credit the photographer who took the photo. If you own the photo full out, you are welcome to put your own name/company if you want. Be sure to remember to put accreditation. This is considered common professional etiquette. Plus, if you don't credit the photographer properly, that person might contact and reprimand you to do so.

The title of your photo should be in the caption you want to show under it. It should appear like this...

Brad McEntire in his one-person show Robert's Eternal Goldfish [credit: Audacity Theatre Lab]

Do not send press photos titled "photo-1" or "pic1" or "IMG_1232." It is unhelpful and amateurish.

Why send in hi-res digital photos? Because, you want good art to be put with the stories people write about you and because you don't want them using some pixelated photos of you they found somewhere on the internet (podcasters, bloggers and other newer media, in particular, unfortunately sometimes do this. They will sometimes raid your Facebook for a simple photo).

Ideally, you want a whole smattering of photos because press outlets love receiving and then using different images than their competitors. So, a good variety of images can only help you. It might even be worth hiring a professional photographer to take some really good photos of you and your show.

If you have a professional photographer take photos for you, make sure you have the rights to use the photos for promotion. Also, be sure to properly credit the photographer whenever you use the picture.

* Hi-Res means High Resolution. Hi-Res is a photo at least 6" x 4" (or 1260 x 960 pixel dimensions image size). This is the minimum. Don't make any photo smaller than this.

☐ Biography

A biography, or *bio* for short, is a write-up about you and your background as a performer. The only advice I would specify when putting together a bio is to only keep relevant information. Media folks, or anyone else for that matter, do not need to know every play you have ever performed in or every workshop you have ever taken. Stick to stuff that establishes your credibility and makes you seem likable.

Highlight what qualifies you to be presenting your solo show. Maybe you have extensive training in the theatre, or background as a writer or performer. Maybe you have years of exposure to the subject matter of your solo show. Maybe you have won awards for this show or others you have created. Maybe you have some other unique aspect about yourself that gives you credibility.

You may also want to include something interesting about yourself in the bio. It humanizes you and can help present you as an engaging person. It is a point of connection and can make people curious about you. Be careful here. You may love dogs, for example, but people don't necessarily need to know that unless it pertains in some way to the show you are presenting.

Ideally, you should prepare three (3) different versions of your bio, each of varying length, and save them in a file on your computer.

- Full one (one page max) - summarizes who you are and what you are about

- short one (one paragraph) - just the big stuff

- one sentence (you'd be surprised how often this can come in handy)

Last, make sure you read all the versions of your bios out loud. Assume interviewers, journalists, arts bloggers and podcasters are going to use your bios verbatim, so make sure it sounds clear and engaging.

☐ Videos (or links to them)

You should have two (2) "promo" videos in your arsenal for each show.

- The first is a short promotional video, like a teaser. Maybe 45 seconds to a minute and half in length. The first 15-20 seconds is a great place to put a really engaging moment from your piece or quick montage of the show set to music. The goal is to hook the viewer's attention right off the bat. This is the video that you circulate the most on social media.

- The second video is a longer one of a few minutes. It should hook the viewer's attention, too, but give a bit more context about your show. Maybe in the middle have a quick "Q-and-A" where you answer some questions about your show as direct address to the camera. You can describe what you hope audiences take away from your show or the origins of your ideas behind the show. Follow this with a solid snippet or two from your show and end on either audience reactions or maybe an overlay of good pull quotes.

☐ **Links to big/ representative online interviews (web and podcast)**

This shows you have been newsworthy in some way already. Just put in the links. No need to put pull quotes from other sources directly in your press kit, since journalists and so on will not be able to use them for their own pieces.

☐ **Contact information**

Include phone, email, your website URL as well as social media links. You do not need to put a mailing address. You want the press to be able to contact you quickly and easily.

These last two are optional...

☐ **List of Awards You've Won**

Won a few Best of Fest Awards? Belonged to some notable residencies? Won a well-known grant? Performed at a prestigious theatre? Would people recognize you from an appearance in a television show, commercial or movie? If you have racked up too many accolades or they didn't fit in your bio, you might dedicate a full page to list them.

☐ **List of interview topics/questions**

If you want an interviewer to cover certain topics, give them a list. If you want to go further, give them the exact questions you want to be asked. They may not do it, but they'll know it is important to your message. Or they may just incorporate a few of the questions you suggest into their own interview. Interviews don't have to be 100% surprise.

Now, put all text elements in Word DOC or a TXT file for easy cut and pasting. You can use PDFs for things that wouldn't normally be cut-and-pasted, such as list of awards, but you should insert working hyperlinks into any PDFs to places where basic information can be straight lifted by press people. Journalists and media folks love cut-and-paste... saves time when a deadline is fast approaching.

Gather all these press kit elements, make them presentable (and, yeah, spell check everything!), then put them in a single folder on your computer. Zip that folder and then put it on your website. You can also put the individual elements as separate sub-pages on your website as well. Just keep it simple.

I would recommend putting these files not just on your website, but also on a small flashdrive. It will rarely happen, but you'll have it to hand out, on request, to reviewers that show up to critique your show.

Do you need a physical press kit? No, I don't think so. Practically, I would say it couldn't hurt, but it is just added expense you don't need. I used to print out full color pages and put them in a nice folder along with a digital version of the press kit on an enclosed CD. I can't imagine handing someone a CD nowadays. Do they even make computers that have CD drives these days?

A flashdrive with your EPK on it as a back-up should be enough. I haven't actually handed out a physical press kit, like in a folder, since 2005.

A press kit is, admittedly, usually thought of as an old-fashioned tool of promotion, but I think it can and should be thought of in a different light for contemporary performers. The true value of a press kit nowadays is that it makes you, the performer, get all of your promotional materials together, fluidly and dependably, in one place. You will then have them on hand when needed.

You have probably already noticed, but many of the things you will be gathering for your EPK are also things you'll need for your website. It is sort of a two birds with one stone scenario.

A solid press kit will brand you as a professional. If you make it easy for people to share the word about you they just might do so.

An Email List

You have now created a show and you are now performing it somewhere. The best way to tell people about it is through an email list. This is the third component of what I think is a really functional, basic marketing platform.

Having a direct connection to a potential audience member's inbox gives the performer a way to communicate in a personal, compelling way. The goal is to have these audience members come see a show or two and become interested, maybe even avid *followers* of you and your work. Followers eventually may, of course, become *fans* when they see how awesome your shows are.

"Wait," you might be thinking, "Isn't email kind of passé? It seems so old-school compared to social media."

Yeah, it is kind of old-school. It is not as popular or as social as Pinterest, Facebook, Twitter, Instagram, YouTube, Tik Tok and whatever other social media is just around the corner. What it lacks in popularity, email makes up for with efficiency.

And like having your own website as a home base instead of depending solely on social media sites, you control it. You aren't beholden to the whims of the algorithms on a social media platform.

I remember the fans I once had on MySpace (long before I started doing solo shows). There wasn't a huge amount, but it was a respectable starting point. Well, MySpace owned their data, not me, and then, when everyone migrated off of MySpace, I lost contact with many of those people.

Facebook? Same deal. Facebook owns the data, and they too can disappear or change algorithms of who sees what. Or, as it seems to be happening, it gets too crowded and noisy. People opt out of paying attention to Facebook, or some other social media thing. This happens more frequently than you may realize. A new thing comes along and everyone jumps over to it and kind of disregards the older social media thing.

Also, statistics regularly show that only a very small percentage of people actually see your updates on Facebook (or any other social media site). So if you have important news to announce, your mailing list is your best bet to reach a lot of your potential audience base. Facebook can still (currently) be useful and I'll touch on how it can a bit later, but the point is, it is Facebook's platform, not yours. You are allowed to use it, but only on the terms laid down by that corporation.

Twitter? Same issue with data, and tweets only last for a few hours, so again, it's hard to tell how many of your followers actually see your updates.

Ultimately, though social media sites are great tools for interacting with current fans and finding new ones, you will want to get them signed-up to your mailing list so you can stay in touch with your fans over the long-term, regardless of which social media site is popular at the time.

If you make an email list, you control it. You built it, so you own it. This means you have direct access to your followers' inboxes from anywhere. No matter how much marketing a festival or theatre is doing for you, you still have the option and capability to turn on your own computer, open up your email list and send everybody a message yourself.

If you nurture your email list with compelling content and protect your followers from spam, they will reward you with paying attention and maybe even taking the time to come see your show (or at the least, helping you spread the word).

Okay, but How Do I Build an Email List?

Fifteen years ago, I remember sending emails out 50 at a time on Hotmail and hoping the SPAM filter would let them through. It took hours - sometimes days - to send the same message out to a couple of hundred people. Email has come a long way since then.

Nowadays, there are web-hosted email platforms like MailChimp (my favorite), iContact, Aweber or Constant Contact. There will probably be different ones by the time this book gets out. These are way more effective than personal email clients like Gmail or Outlook. How so? Because software like Gmail, Yahoo! Mail or Outlook does not easily facilitate list building; you have to do it manually. Also, your email will start getting blocked, SPAM reports will spike and your potential followers will become frustrated if there is no easy way to unsubscribe. Let me reiterate, using personal email software like Gmail or Outlook for email marketing is inefficient and likely to violate Federal CAN-SPAM laws.

After selecting an email list service, you need to gather email addresses. First thing, follow the directions in the email list service on how to make a "subscribe to my mailing list" link to put on your website. Put this prominently on the home/landing page of your website. Next, reach out to your closest friends and family through your personal email software and direct them to sign up for your mailing list. After these two things are done, gathering emails becomes sort of a long game.

Pay attention to anyone who shows interest in you or your show. It could be the organizers and staff of a festival who email you, or folks who like a post about your show on Facebook. Contact these people back and invite them to sign up for your mailing list. Send them the link. You can also offer to sign them up yourself. But, and this is important, you must have a person's permission before you add them to your email list. Putting someone on your list if they did not sign up usually leads to a quick unsubscribe and you becoming a mild annoyance to the same people you want to attend your shows. Plus, it is just plain impoliteness to add someone who didn't ask..

Since people must voluntarily sign up for your email list, it has another major benefit. Once people give you their email address, they're letting you know that they *want* to hear about your work, that they *want* to know about your next show and so on.

That's an incredibly powerful thing, and those email addresses should be treated like gold.

On an episode of the WTF podcast with Marc Maron, Kevin Hart was interviewed about his days as a young comedian just starting out. Hart talks about how he used his email list to sell-out shows early in his career.

When Hart started out, he did the comedy club circuit four years in a row, and at every show, he collected email addresses from audience members by leaving cards on each table with the message "Kevin Hart needs to know who you are". People would leave their email addresses, and after his set Kevin made sure to get the cards back from these audience members before they left the club.

His assistant would then log all the email addresses into a spreadsheet organized by city, so the next time Kevin was performing there, he would reach out to every person individually to invite them to his show. This personal touch helped to sell out his shows and build a loyal fan base that follows him to this day.

If you find you are touring to the same cities, returning to a particular festival year after year, play the same venue show after show, then it is a good idea to have an email list specific to that place.

Over time, your email list will grow and grow. As long as you keep it updated (weeding out continually unresponsive addresses) and touch base every so often, then this direct means of sharing news about you and your shows with potential followers will serve as an effective backbone in your marketing platform.

Using Your Email List

What do I put in the emails I send out and how often?

The obvious answer is to send out info when you have something you want people to know about. If you have a show or project coming up, then send out an email about it.

What about when you are between projects?

Some folks, in other fields, particularly internet marketing types who have YouTube channels or are trying to sell courses all the time, will have newsletters and send out an email to their entire list multiple times a week. Some even daily. This seems a bit much to me.

On the other hand, some people only send an email out once a year. I recommend somewhere between once a week and never. A weekly email seems too close to SPAM to me, but on the other hand, you don't want to completely disappear off people's radars between gigs.

When I am performing regularly (like when something like a worldwide pandemic is not going on) I send out emails leading up to my shows, of course, but in slow times I still touch base with my email list quarterly. I find that is roughly enough for folks to stay aware of me, but not so much that I blitzkrieg their inboxes. Sometimes it is just a quick behind-the-scenes glimpse at a show I am developing, or a short write-up about fun stuff I did in a specific city at a recent fringe festival.

Most of the time, however, the content of my emails include information about the upcoming show I'm working on. It usually has the same basic info I would put on my website; complete with links for purchasing tickets, maps and directions to the venue, maybe parking information if that is relevant or links to particularly good reviews. The emails are usually a little more personal and conversational that the information I would put on the website, but I make sure to include all the information someone might need about the show.

Oh, and like everything else, I proof-read to make sure I spell everything correctly.

Let's do a little thought experiment...

Let's say I am attending a festival in Scranton, Pennsylvania. It is halfway across the country from where I live in Dallas, a long way from my home turf. Let's say I only know five people in Scranton. I email each of these people on my email list and say, "Hey, I'm bringing my solo show [insert name of show] to the Scranton Fringe Festival next month. Please help me spread the word. I am proud of this show and it has been a hit everywhere I've taken it. I'd love to share it with as many audience members as possible in Scranton. If you will share it on Facebook, Twitter and maybe email a few friends to let them know about the show, I would genuinely appreciate it. And, of course, I hope I see you at the show. Make sure you stay around after the closing curtain so I can say hello in person and thank you for your support."

Now, this might not bring in even a single audience member, but then again, it might bring fifteen or twenty. It could exponentially increase the number of audience members to my show. Even if only two people show up because of these quick emails I sent out, that's two more audience members than I would have had. That makes the few minutes I spent on it worth it. Plus, I potentially have an opportunity to get more email addresses for next time.

Managing an email list and sending out updates and newsletters may take some getting used to at first, but I do believe over time, it will be a valuable resource to help you market your shows. A book that helped me that I can recommend is *Newsletter Ninja* by Tammi Labrecque.

So, here's the take away for this section: marketing is both learnable and mandatory. Creating a marketing platform will make spreading the word about your show much easier than it would otherwise be. A marketing platform includes a clean and easy to navigate website, an Electronic Press Kit for your show and an email list.

Before I move on from marketing, I want to touch on a few other things that may help you get the word out about your show, particularly how to talk about your show in person and how social media can be really useful.

A Word About In-Person Marketing

The world of theatre - particularly solo performance - is like many other things... it is about relationships. Eventually, you'll reach a point where people want to work with you because they know you and your work. And they like you. You'll be invited to present your show at venues and functions and so on. Audiences will talk with you and find you engaging and take a chance and go see your work. Fellow artists hope you will be at the same festival they will be at. They'll start to follow your work. And the best way to get to know and like people is to spend time with them outside of that short time you are in front of them on stage while actually presenting your show.

When people approach you, take a moment to talk about your show. Promote your work. Be nice. Be engaging. Make others look good. Make yourself worthy of being talked about. This is a particular kind of in-person, face-to-face marketing traditionally called *networking*.

Oh sure, you need to be good, be professional, and not be a punk-ass jerk. But, just like everywhere else in the working world, people want to work with and watch people they find likeable and engaging. And if directors/ producers/ fellow performers/ audience members can get to know you a bit and like you outside of the brief times when you're onstage (i.e. in the lobby or at the bar after the show), you increase the possibility of them coming to see you the *next time* you are on stage.

Some theatre artists I speak to — playwrights, designers, directors and performers — don't like all this in-person marketing. Networking is a dirty word to them. They think it's beneath them, or too difficult, that their art should speak for itself, and they should be judged solely on the merits of their work. Maybe they feel they are naturally too shy, too introverted, too socially awkward to talk themselves up. Maybe they don't want to bother people because they think talking to people equals bothering them. Maybe they are fearful that they won't be able to tell where the line is between being proud of their own work and bragging about themselves.

But here's the deal: networking and marketing are part of the whole thing. For solo performers who are the creators as well as the production teams behind their shows, it is part of the entire endeavor. No one is going to automatically do it for you. That is not going to happen. You must be the biggest champion for your show. You must be a solo performer on stage and off. You are the administrator of your own little theatre company of one. Sometimes, we want part of a thing without the other parts. Solo performers should just get used to idea that marketing and networking are just an automatic part of the whole crazy thing.

I do not wish to be too harsh here, but if you are not prepared to market yourself to some degree, maybe solo performance is not the format for you. Heck, maybe performance, in general, is not for you.

Talking About Yourself, In-Person (Especially To Press and Media People)

Did you ever notice how movie actors conduct themselves on press junkets? Or how they come across when being interviewed on talk shows? If you pay attention, most celebrities who need to sell something (movies, music, books, politics, executives, etc.) conduct themselves in a certain manner. They are likeable or relatable and maybe even charming. They have a studied air of being both at-ease, but also very aware of themselves. They are sometimes humorous without being overly clever. They are presentable, even attractive, almost all of the time. They stay on message about selling themselves or their message/product. This professional and engaging manner is not necessarily inauthentic, but it has a degree of polish to it. Celebrities come off this way because they have often received media training.

What is media training? Media training is a type of communication training for people who plan to have interactions with media outlets. This training prepares individuals to represent themselves, a product, a brand or a company to the media by teaching them how to discuss relevant topics in an engaging and professional way.

Do I think solo performers should go out of their way to get extensive media training? No. I do, however, believe most performers should put some thought in how they come across to other people, especially press and media folks, when they talk about their work.

Remember when I stated earlier there were three areas to focus on when marketing your solo performance? You can focus on selling yourself as a performer, you can focus on selling the content of your show or you can focus on selling a combination of the two. Media training allows you to do any and all of these, in person, smoothly and efficiently.

You may find classes in media training, either in-person or online. These are usually tailored for politicians or executives, but a lot of the lessons and techniques carry over for performers. I have found reading a few books about developing personal engagement can up your game substantially. Most of them are filled with little techniques and common sense reminders of how to talk to people and present oneself in a positive fashion.

In her book, for example, *The Charisma Myth* author Olivia Fox Cabane explains that charisma is not a gift some people are just naturally born with and others are not. Charisma is a skill that can be practiced. She cites three important behaviors for becoming more personally engaging: presence (the ability to focus, listen and engage), power (own the space you are in, confidence that can be backed up) and warmth (being genuinely kind, courteous and caring).

*NOTE ABOUT BEING INTERVIEWED: You don't have to answer the exact same way to every similar question you are asked from interview to interview, but make sure your message is consistent. Also, **be interesting**. This means being personable and engaging (This is something arts journalist-turned-solo performer Elaine Liner continually emphasizes).*

Remember, press folks are trying to sell their own products and you are the content. Help them sell you so they can help you sell your show.

See the resources list at the end of this book for suggested books about "media training."

CHAPTER 9 – MARKETING PART 2

In the previous section I went over setting up a platform. This will serve as a foundation for marketing your show. But what about the process of actually marketing when you head off to a festival or to a venue in another city?

First, here are a few things you may need. The content for these things will come from the press release you already wrote, the blurbs you already worked out and the photos you have already taken for your website.

Postcards and Posters

It is a good idea to have postcards or flyers to hand out. These should have a neat full-color image on the front. You can make your own graphic or have one made. I sometimes use a photo from the show and place some text on it, such as the title of the show.

On the back, usually in black and white because it is cheaper than doing both sides in color, I'll put a very short blurb, my name and the website where people can find out more information about the show.

As I mentioned earlier, I'll often leave room on the back to put a mailing label with specific production information. On the labels, which I just run off on my desktop printer, I put the venue address, performance dates and times, and a link for purchasing tickets. Some fringe festivals require placing the logo for that festival on all promotional material, so I'll put it on the label as well.

I order these postcards several weeks before I head off to a festival or venue at an online printing service. I usually use VistaPrint, but there are a bunch of them (I have also used Modern Postcard and Moo in the past). Don't wait until the last minute when ordering postcards. Rush shipping is more expensive. Allow for possible hold-ups in the postal system, too.

I make sure I save the front postcard image and information I placed on the back of the postcard on my backup flashdrive. If I need to run off more postcards while on the road, I'll pop into a copy shop and have a few dozen printed off on cardstock.

There will also be some opportunities from time to time to put up posters. This is a gradually disappearing mode of promotion, but there is some places on fences and walls in some cities where putting up unsolicited advertising is still allowed. Currently, for many fringe festivals, postering is expected.

Besides outdoor spaces, posters can also be placed on community bulletin boards in shops or in the front windows of local businesses. If you want your poster put up in the front window of a business, go in and ask and employee if it would be okay. Sometimes they will let you do it yourself, but usually they will have you leave it with them and they will place it in the front window for you. Take some tape with you, just in case.

I usually make the poster just a bigger version of the postcard. Of course, all the information needs to be on the front of a poster. I also save that image on my backup flashdrive. Make sure you use the same fonts and design elements that you used on your other marketing materials.

Make sure you make your poster a standard size. 11 x 17 inches is what I find is the unofficial standard at most fringe and solo festivals. Make sure you orient the poster vertically and not horizontally. 11 x 17 inches also allows you to run off more prints at a copy shop if needed.

If you are headed to a festival, spend the first day or two after arriving, preferably before the bulk of your shows take place, and go around putting up posters and dropping off postcards in the lobbies at all the venues. At some big fests, such as the Edinburgh Fringe, you can hire people to both put up posters for you and even hand out postcards and flyers for you.

Talk Up Your Show to Normal Folks

I went over learning how to speak in an engaging fashion about your show a little earlier. In that section I was focusing on speaking with the press in a more official way. I mentioned how useful media training might be for helping performers to talk about their shows. But what about talking about your show in casual settings? To regular people or potential audience members?

I have witnessed the following scenario play out many times over the years. A potential audience member asks the performer what their piece of theatre is about. The performer's expression shows a mixture of boredom and annoyance before he or she answers with some vague sentence. The performer offers nothing to really hook the potential audience member. The performer way undersells their show, sometimes they even come off like they are a little bothered by the question.

To reiterate from earlier… Champion Your Own Show! You should be excited about your work. You should be excited to share this work. Your implicit excitement can make others excited, too.

I have also met a lot of performers who have developed a sort of elevator pitch about their shows. They have it down to a quick and clever (or mysterious, or bizarre, etc.) blurb that they can recite to people curious to know about their show.

You don't need to overdo it, but don't be timid about talking about your work. You might consider yourself a shy or introverted person, but this is an instance when you should put yourself forward. You can still be sincere and quiet if that is your bag, but don't clam up. Get people interested in seeing your stuff.

By the same token, if you are approached after the show and an audience member shows interest, do not be dismissive. If they say good show and you don't think it went well, just smile and say thanks. Show this person gratitude. They came to see your art.

One question I get a lot from audience members is "where did you get the idea for this show?" I also hear, "Did this come from your real life?" You know what I do when people ask one of these reoccurring questions? I answer them. I don't let on that I have been presented with the same question over and over again. I accept their interest and reciprocate with cheerful engagement.

The most difficult thing I have found is bringing up my show when no one asks about it. Sometimes I get around this by wearing a t-shirt with the title of my show on it (I make these online on sites like Spreadshirt). Really, I just listen. I try to recognize organic places in a conversation when I can tell someone about my show, or better yet lead them to ask about it.

A good friend of mine and fellow solo performer named John Michael is the best person I have ever seen at approaching random people and engaging them about his show. He is hella out-going and simply walks up and directly says some funny or controversial sentence to hook people. One of his shows is called *Meatball Séance*. In it he cooks his deceased mother's meatball recipe live, onstage, with the help of an audience volunteer. The aim of the show is to have the audience rethink their customary reactions to the death of loved ones. John Michael will approach a person on the street or in a theatre lobby and say, "I need your help to bring my mom back from the dead."

This will usually prompt the person to ask what he is talking about and then a brief conversation forms. He tells them about his show, gives them a postcard and has left a distinct impression. It helps that he is puppy-like in his enthusiasm and fearless in approaching pretty much anyone.

"I feel people are stopped from interacting because they are too worried about being inappropriate," John Michael says. "Not me."

While I'm mentioning John Michael, he also said something once that stuck with me. He said, "The way you market a show reflects how you are as a performer."

I agree with this. If you are a professional on the stage, you are likely a professional behind-the-scenes as well. And vice versa.

So, don't be afraid to talk to people about your show, particularly if they show curiosity. If there is a way to organically invite people out to see your show, try to be aware of it and use the opportunity. Champion your show. If someone asks about your work, respond the way you'd want to someone to respond to you.

Request a Media List

One thing I have found useful, especially if I am touring out-of-town to a far off venue or festival is to request a media list. A media list is used by the person or department at an organization to help market events. It is literally a list of contacts in the press and media who one should get the word out to.

Media lists include local arts journalists, critics, reviewers, even arts bloggers and such.

This information is useful. It says where and sometimes, how, to send press releases, story pitches and so on.

If you are not from that city, this is particularly helpful for getting the word out about your show.

Contact the organizers of the festival or the staff at a theatre you might be heading to several weeks before your show. More often than not, they will be willing to send you this info so you can market yourself.

Social Media

Social media changes too fast for me to go into details about it in this book. I'm sure some of the references I have already made up to this point will age like expired milk.

My thoughts about using social media to market are 1.) it can't hurt and 2.) don't let it be the ONLY way you market your show.

Social media is a decent way for letting people know about events. For some potential audience members, the primary way they find out about stuff happening in the world is through social media. So, don't ignore social media as a way to market your show. Just don't rely on it as the only way you market your show.

Typically, I make a Facebook event for my show for each run it has. If I plan to do the show more than a few times, I make a separate "Page" for it on Facebook. I have not done it myself, but I see a lot of solo performers create a "show account" on Instagram as well. They then link that Instagram account to the Facebook page they made so they can post on both simultaneously.

During the run I will update either Facebook or Instagram (or both) with pull quotes from audience feedback or reviews, show photos and video snippets. The more activity and "noise" the more it seems like the show is a sort of big deal. The more a potential audience member comes across it in their social media feeds, the more of an impression it can potentially make. I find the inverse also true. The less noise that is made about the show, the more it kind of fades into the woodwork, so to speak. Visibility does kind of equal relevance, at least in the terms of social media's attention economy.

With mixed results I have also used Facebook ads, especially for traveling to cities I haven't been to before. Admittedly, I am exceedingly lazy about checking the analytics afterwards to see if they were really beneficial.

I will usually place the best promo video on YouTube and link it as needed leading up to a production run as well.

That is pretty much the extent of the social media I use. If you have a following on TikTok, use it. Active on Twitter, use it. If you have an old-school following on, I don't know, LiveJournal or Tumblr, use those.

As I was born of the generation that bridged the analogue and the digital, I look at social media as either purely social or as tools for promotion. The mixing of business and personal on social media is personally bothersome to me, so I self-limit my use of it. However, I realize many people are way more savvy than I am on social media and really do accept being sold to on the same platform they see pictures of their cousin's summer vacation.

Really, it is up to you. Use social media as much or as little as you want. There are a lot of resources on YouTube and across the internet to find out how to use social media very effectively as a marketing tool.

Let me reiterate, however, that you should not ONLY use social media as the sole means of marketing your show. Algorithms are constantly changing and the reach of these apps are way more limited than most people understand… at least as a marketing tool for live productions.

My suggestion is to use your EPK, website and mailing list as foundational marketing tools and then think of social media as supplemental. In fact, all these things can work together really well. However, there is only a finite amount of time and energy available to each of us. Use it wisely.

Last Word on Marketing

So what if you follow all the things I laid out it the previous few sections of this book? You go to great lengths with a tremendous amount of work. You have a great title for your show. You create a great, informative and easy to navigate website. You put together an EPK complete with a succinct press release, photos of your show and catchy promo videos. You start an email list and make periodic newsletters. You think up engaging ways to interact with people in real life and engage them in organic conversations about your show. You get flyers or postcards made and hand them out liberally. You get posters made and hang them up everywhere. You contact the venue or festival and request a media list and send out press releases and story pitches about your show. Maybe you are invited to sit down for radio or podcast interviews or get a profile feature in a local alt-weekly. Maybe you do all this and more.

And you still get small audiences.

Unfortunately, this can happen. I have been at this for years and I am still flummoxed by how sometimes I can have a full house and sometimes I can perform for five people…at the same festival. Marketing is still mysterious to me and it seems to become even more so as live performance, as a whole, struggles to keep a foothold in an increasingly digital world.

Admittedly, I come at all of this from the perspective of a theatre-maker, not a marketing professional. So, everything I know I've had to learn bit by bit as I have progressed and I'm sure I will continue to learn as I keep going.

I acknowledge that I am working in an art form that inherently has a smaller viewership than other forms, such as television, movies, radio, podcasts mainstream publishing or online media. That said, I always consider it my duty to give my show the best shot it has at being seen by as many people as it can. This means I do my best to market my work as thoroughly as I can. Most of the time it helps draw in an audience. Sometimes I feel like I am yelling at the wind and nothing seems to come of all the hard work.

Either way, if I don't make an effort to get the word out about my show, I can be sure that it will slip completely under the radar. Not marketing is a surefire way to have low audience numbers. Once again, marketing is mandatory. It is the responsibility of the solo performer to champion his or her own work and to get the word out. As I stated earlier, nobody will show up for a show they don't even know is happening.

CHAPTER 10 – KEEP GOING

Now you have your show, you have been performing it and you have taken it to a few places. Now what? Keep going.

One of the truly wonderful aspects of touring a solo show to different places over a long span of time is that it offers opportunities for the show to grow and develop. As a performer you will make many tiny discoveries about the piece. It will change and deepen as time goes by.

Performing my shows in different venues, in front of different audiences, has presented me with the opportunity to see my own show in a new light over and over again. A joke or reference I made in the original version might become dated or passé. I see hidden themes emerge. I realize the emphasis on different points can change. I really like the organic evolution of a show as it is presented over and over again over time.

Also, we as people change. I know I have changed over the years, both as a person and as a performer. So, the piece and what it means to me also changes.

I spotlight this continual development aspect because in a lot of other regards, theatre produced on a smaller level doesn't afford this sort of opportunity. Unless you are performing eight shows a week on Broadway or at an Off-Broadway theatre, or you are part of a professional touring company, nowadays many productions only last a few weeks.

If you got cast in a local community theatre, middle-level or even regional theatre you would rehearse a few weeks then run the show for several weekends and that would be that. You would move on to the next production. You only *live* with the show for a limited span of time.

With a self-produced touring solo show, you can perform it for as long as you want. I have performed my show *Robert's Eternal Goldfish*, off and on, for the last nine years... and it still has a few more engagements in it before I finally put it up on the shelf.

Finding Performance opportunities

One of the big questions I faced early on was "where do I take my show?"

There are a bunch of opportunities to perform a one-person show, but unless you know where to look for these opportunities, it isn't always clear. In this section I want to offer a few suggestions of places to find out about venues, festivals and other opportunities to perform your show.

The first thing I think of when I create a new show is fringe festivals. If you are not familiar with the term "fringe" festivals are performing arts events that last from one long weekend to several weeks. They are produced outside of major mainstream institutions and are, according to the MacMillian Dictionary, "often small-scale and non-traditional in style or subject matter."

Some fringe festivals are curated, or "juried" and hand-select the acts featured in the festival. Some are "unjuried," meaning the acts are chosen by a lottery system. Fringe fests usually happen in big cities, happen annually (most in the summer) and some have hundreds of acts. The well-established ones bring in enthusiastic, recurring audiences to check out each year's fresh programming.

Fringes have a producing organization that oversees programming, ticketing and overall promotion (meaning they market the festival as a whole). Often, but not always, the producing organization will handle venue rentals, as well as filling tech, venue management and board op positions. They will partner with local businesses to offer discounts to performers and audiences. Sometimes they will even help performers find accommodation in town, often connecting them with local performing artists who can offer a spare couch or guest room (this is called "billeting" as I discussed earlier).

Fringe is a performing arts tradition that started in Edinburgh, Scotland in 1947 when eight performing groups were excluded from the mainstream annual arts festival. They decided to perform anyway, finding inexpensive or free venues on the fringes of the city. A journalist noted that some interesting things were happening "around the fringe" of the main festival and the term stuck.

Side-note here: This origin story always bothered me. It makes it sound like a bunch of party-crashers who interrupted an event they weren't invited to. I am reminded of an incident I faced as a producer of a festival.

In 2016 I was producing the Dallas Solo Fest, an annual arts event that brought together eight performers from around North America to Dallas, Texas. Each performer was presenting several performances of his or her original solo show over the two weekend-long festival. I held the festival at the tiny Margo Jones Theatre in Fair Park. The Margo Jones is so named because it is the place the Regional Theatre movement started in 1947, by the director Margo Jones. Fair Park is so named because it is the location of the huge Texas State Fair every autumn. The Park has lots of buildings and various attractions year-round.

On the Saturday of the first weekend of the Dallas Solo Fest, an event I was producing, I showed up a few hours before the first performances of the day and noticed more traffic than usual through the Park. I ducked into the building and began preparing the space for the evening. That evening about fifteen minutes before the first performance of the evening, I heard a loud band start playing… right in front of the theatre!

They had speakers and people were standing around dancing. Out of the crowd about twenty older women in matching t-shirts bopped up to the area in between the band and the onlookers. They began dancing in unison.

I turned to my associate producer and with a mournful look asked, "Great. What do we do about a bunch of dancing grandmas?!"

The management at Fair Park had booked the band in front of the theatre, not taking into account the enormous sound-bleed. They had mentioned nothing about it to me. And, of course, since it was nearly 7:00 pm on a Saturday, anyone I might have called to help resolve the unexpected issue was no longer in their office. I thought about unplugging the band's power and shooing all the party-goers away, but that seemed too harsh. It wasn't the band's fault. It wasn't the dancing grandmas' fault.

In the end, I had to profusely apologize to the performer who had flown halfway across the country to present his show in my festival. I also apologized directly to the evening's audience. I offered them all a heavily reduced admission price for that performance (though only one person took me up on it... that was a cool, forgiving audience).

That was one of many issues I dealt with producing that festival at the Park. In hindsight, I can laugh about it and, admittedly, airing it out here in this book helps.

So, I have little sympathy for the groups that did not get into that arts festival in Edinburgh back in 1947. That they decided to have their own festival right on top of the bigger festival seems equivalent to someone spending lots of money, energy and time planning a wedding and then showing up to the venue to see that some inconsiderate squatter decided to throw a birthday party that day in the same place at the same time.

Fringe fests are good outlets for solo performances. They usually have a scrappy, DIY or indie vibe. The audiences that frequent fringes are often open-minded, adventurous and curious. Ticket prices are kept low to allow wide accessibility.

The performer will pay a festival fee in advance (usually several hundred dollars), but pocket a large percentage of ticket sales. Sometimes the performer even collects 100% of ticket sales income.

As I mentioned earlier, this book covers a large amount of performance opportunities. Attending fringe fests is a big piece of that pie, but by all means not the only one. In addition, there are many, many things specific to performing at fringes that are way beyond the scope of this book. Luckily, there are a lot of online resources and other materials if you are interested in attending fringe festivals.

To find out about the Fringe Fests and when they open submissions, particularly if you are in North America, I recommend you check out CAFF, or the Canadian Association of Fringe Festivals. CAFF is an international organization that promotes and sets guidelines for fringe theatre throughout North America. The CAFF website [http://fringefestivals.com] has an extensive list of annual fringe fests around Canada and the United States and is a good resource.

Beyond official "fringe" festivals there are a lot of smaller unofficial fringe-like festivals. Sometimes a theatre fest will call itself a fringe even though they are not officially such an event. For example, in Texas where I live, at the time of this writing, there are festivals in Houston, Tyler and Ft. Worth that bill themselves as "fringes" though they use the moniker rather loosely. These events have similar structures and organizing principles as official fringe festivals, just on much smaller scales.

Another outlet that might be considered would be the rising number of "solo fests." These events especially feature one-person shows. Some run like fringe fests, some with very different organizing structures. I produced one of these solo fests in Dallas between 2014 and 2019. At the time of this writing the United Solo Theatre Fest in New York, Solo Flights in Aspen, Colorado and the SoLow Fest in Philadelphia are further examples of these sorts of festivals.

Another outlet to consider, especially if you are more established as a solo performer, is performing arts centers. Most major cities have large performing arts centers (PACs) that have multiple performance spaces housed in a large facility. Members subscribe for a year of programming and are offered a schedule of concerts, dance recitals, musicals and other cultural performances.

It is worth contacting the Programming Manager at PACs to see if they need supplemental programming for their smaller spaces. You never know, they might be looking for something to break up (or rather, pad out) the usual schedule of Asian acrobats, *Wicked* and Steve Martin playing banjo. I have seen solo performers Mike Daisey, Eric Bogosian and John Leguizamo on stage at the PAC in Dallas.

You may also want to look into performing snippets of your show at open mics, approaching community or regional theatres, making proposals to comedy clubs (if your show is funny) or even renting out a venue on your own to present a run of your show.

Making Money as a Solo Performer

Real talk... I do not know anyone who has gotten rich performing solo shows. It is just not one of those fields people enter expecting to get outrageously wealthy. However, there are a few ways to make solo performing financially worth your time.

The first thing you'll notice once you begin creating then rehearsing and touring your shows is that it doesn't need to cost a fortune to put the thing together. There is one person to pay. The solo performer is also the playwright. Most solo shows do not have extensive sets and costumes and other technical elements. They can, of course, but what I am getting at is that they don't have to.

You can hire a director to work with you. You can hire a script consultant or a public relations firm or a tour manager or a stage manager. You can bring in musicians. You can hire graphic designers to make your marketing materials. You can hire a web designer to create your website. You can hire people that will handle your social media for you. You can hire people to hand out flyers for you, people to put your posters up. You can hire any and all these people.

But you don't have to.

As I have, hopefully, illustrated throughout this book, solo performing can be done by a lone performer. Is it more difficult than working with a whole production team? Heck yeah it is. But it is not impossible. It is just a matter of, over time, acquiring the necessary skill sets.

So, the first way to make solo performance financially feasible is to lower your overhead. Solo performance is, comparatively speaking, a pretty economical production method. Look for ways to save in production costs. The less you spend the less you put your budget in the red. The less in the red, then the faster you can start making your money back by performing.

Doesn't the acquisition of new skills and writing and rehearsing cost time and energy? Yes. A great amount. But the production process doesn't necessarily need to cost a lot of money. Admittedly, it is a trade-off, but still, there it is.

The second way I find that I have profited off my solo shows is that I very rarely perform the entire show for free. Or absolutely free. I sometimes will do portions of it for charity events or open mics. However, if I am doing the full out theatrical show, there ought to be tickets sold and I should be getting a cut of those ticket sales. And that cut should be as high as possible. Or I have worked out a flat fee of some kind with the venue or producing organization. A contract is drawn up and everything stays above board.

I have done free performances of my shows on very rare occasions, but I always consider the trade-off. I value my time and energy and creative output. So, if I perform for free, then I am probably doing so for some other potential non-monetary benefit. It could be for networking purposes or for a charitable cause I particularly believe in.

I performed at a relatively small, emerging festival in east Texas recently that was hosted by the faculty of a college campus. I put on two performances of a no-tech version of one of my shows. The goal was to make connections there so I can later come out and teach a workshop or perhaps even present a future performance with full ticket sales.

What I am getting at here is that you should be mindful of the value you are offering. I believe this is a healthy artistic mindset. Don't undervalue your work. Getting paid to present your show should be the default and then you can make the call on a case by case basis of whether or not you want to offer it for less (or offer less product). It should not be the other way around.

Putting together your show was a lot of work, so don't just give it away. Place real value on yourself and your show. If possible, get paid.

Last, I want to touch on adjacent ways to profit off your solo shows. These include selling merchandise, conducting workshops, applying for grants and even contemporary patronage services like Indiegogo, Kickstarter and Patreon. Even adjacent online activities like YouTube channels and Etsy pages can be tied into your solo show. As long as it initially springs out of your solo performance activities, it goes under the umbrella of money made from solo performance.

"Merch" – short for merchandise - can be stickers, books, t-shirts, caps, mugs, posters, DVDs or really anything. One performer I met years ago sold a series of songs from his show as a link. You bought the link, written on a piece of paper, and it took you to a playlist of his songs online which you could download if you wanted. This was neat because the guy didn't have to travel with any actual physical goods to keep track of.

I have published some of my plays on Amazon and will sometimes set up outside the venue after a show and sell these books.

Several years ago I was performing at a festival in Minnesota. My friend and colleague Martin Dockery was also performing there. I went to see his show (it was wonderful) and after the performance he spread a bunch of DVDs out on the lip of the stage. He set an upside down cap next to them and said they were recordings of shows he had performed in the past. Twenty dollars a disc. Just put the money in the cap. I bought one, a recording of his show *The Bike Trip*. Martin went about thanking audience members for coming to see the show he had just performed. He trusted that people would pay if they took a DVD. I thought it was a wonderful, low-key way of selling merchandise.

I met another performer who sold thumbdrives with a video of the show on it as well as a behind-the-scenes "making of" video, complete with a rather hilarious, fictional interview with a Rolling Stone-like journalist. It also had other supplemental materials (like humorous discarded poster ideas) on it. Again, really clever idea for merch.

It is beyond the scope of this book to go into detail about things like selling ad revenue by starting a YouTube channel, setting up a living room tour or all the different kinds of merch that can be sold. There are resources online for such things. Suffice to say, there are other ways to make money off of the work you do on your solo shows beyond just performing it onstage. Keep this in mind and be as creative about it as you want.

Last, I would like to point out that by this point, if you have assembled an original solo show, tour around and perform it and market it yourself, you have probably acquired a bunch of new skill sets you didn't have before or have strengthened ones you did.

Solo performance may have afforded you a skill set that will make you very competitive in the contemporary marketplace. For instance, you now know how, to some degree or other, to...

- handle scheduling, deadlines, rehearsals and so on.

- edit, format and post online videos, audio, documents, photos, etc.

- design and maintain a website.

- maintain mailing lists.

- keep track of "brand" aesthetic.

- keep on message.

- accept criticism in context and, often, gracefully.

- Forge your own path of progression where none is laid out before you.

- Develop and enforce your own standards of excellence.

- communicate to the press and media.

- copywrite everything from blog posts, to tweets, from media pitches to press releases, and so on.

- get a physical object such as a set piece or article of costume from one location to another.

- keep track of countless details.

- be on time and prepared.

- coordinate travel schedules, accommodations, transportation, etc.

- be courteous in following-up (including sending actual thank you cards on stationary or shout outs on FB).

- work under pressure (Tech! Deadlines!).

- rest when necessary, work harder when necessary.

- celebrate when necessary.

- grow a following.

- make something from scratch where it previously wasn't even imagined!

Notice these skills are up and beyond simply writing and performing your show.

As a market force, then, you are actually something to be reckoned with. You can apply these new skill sets to any other adjacent activities you might desire.

IN CONCLUSION

Now you have created a show from scratch. You are equipped to rehearse and perform that show. You are set up to tour the show around to different venues and even market it yourself.

Now what?

I do not know what the future of solo performance will be. I see encouraging signs when shows like Phoebe Waller-Bridge's *Fleabag* becomes a hit series or when Natalie Palamides manages to turn her show *Nate: A One-Man Show* into a special on Netflix.

By its nature, solo performance is an intimate art form. It may lend itself to cameras and microphones (maybe), but probably won't be playing stadiums and huge rock venues. I mean, it might… but probably not.

As of yet, one-person shows are not playing at high volume mainstream arenas very often. Solo performers often need to have other credits to their name to get their shows into places where they can get it produced as a streamable show or turned into a movie or concert film. I imagine it is easier to get into the offices at Amazon if you also write for television or are a stand-up comedian or known in nationally-airing commercials.

The flip side of fame is also true. Traditionally, most performers who manage to make an impact as solo artists segue their notoriety into other acting of writing gigs. Eric Bogosian didn't keep doing solo performance once he made it onto television. Whoopi Goldberg did not return to solo performance once she made it big. Solo work seems to be a stepping stone to a wider career in higher paying fields. It is not unheard of for popular solo performers to return once in a while. John Leguizamo has returned to the solo stage after years of motion picture acting. Hal Holbrook continued to perform his Mark Twain show for decades despite being an actor on Broadway as well as winning Tony and Emmy Awards.

Perhaps no one has set the bar of what a career in solo performance could be quite like Ruth Draper. Ms. Draper worked exclusively as a solo performer, presenting her original monodramas around the world for years, including multiple royal command performances. She created her own work and presented it with little more than a chair, a shawl and perhaps a small side table. She earned a wage equal to her place in upper class society.

Her body of work numbered over forty pieces, most of which she carried in her head and could slip into at any given time. The reach of her influence, both to those who saw her in person as well as those that heard her recordings, is like a Who's Who of famous performers and writers: Eddie Cantor, John Gielgud, Henry Adams, Marc Connelly, Henry James, Joyce Grenfell, Maurice Chevalier, Edith Wharton, George Bernard Shaw, Agatha Christie, David Mamet, Annette Bening, Lily Tomlin, Charles Busch, Uta Hagen, Mike Nichols, Charles Nelson Reilly, Tom Waits, John Lithgow, and Simon Callow.

Draper performed her own original work exclusively. Famously, novelist Henry James wrote a custom monologue for her, but Draper never performed it. Her "monodramas" were innovative at the time, a step beyond the other solo performers working then. She presented original characters when others were performing excerpts taken from published literature.

Ruth Draper dominated professional solo performance in a career that spanned thirty-five years, from the early 1920s to the mid-1950s. She never segued to film or radio. She didn't become an author or spokesperson. She was an austere, modest woman who enjoyed recognition, but shunned celebrity. She just performed her solo shows. That was it. That was her end goal... solo performance.

And for a time, she did it better than anyone else in the world.

Artist as instigator

I have one final thought I want to leave you with. I believe in artists as instigators.

Too often I have seen genuinely talented people spend their lives doing the work given to them by others. I have seen talented actors laboring away for years selling soft tacos and insurance in commercials or playing bit parts on television shows. I have seen very experienced performers in their older years still doing community theatre productions for want of really juicy, demanding parts to play. I have seen talented writers turn to web series and television and screenplays rather than slog it out writing for the stage.

Traditionally an actor is asked to play roles in other people's works. At best, the actor-for-hire is an interpretive artist. The traditional actor, for the bulk of his or her career, plays parts others have played, in plays written by various playwrights, some alive, some long dead.

The difference between a traditional actor and a generative solo performer is like the difference between musicians who exclusively play covers and singer-songwriters who create the music themselves. One is only called upon to *interpret*, while the other is called upon to *create*. The *creative* artist, in the original sense of the word, is someone who makes something from scratch. A work is brought into existence where nothing had existed before.

I do not think actors should all of the sudden stop being interpretive artists. Who would act in all those multi-cast plays, shows and films? I do think solo performance offers a wonderful alternative. It offers the actor a chance to step out of secondhand creation and be an instigator of their art. An instigator is someone who generates originality and takes responsibility for the execution for that idea from concept to presentation. Solo performers are instigating artists.

The same can be said for playwrights. You can spend a lifetime writing plays for other people to perform and hope that the artists involved can bring it to life with even 50% of what you had in mind. Or, you can take the reins yourself and fashion a play for yourself, a show with a cast of one. You can create a show where your message is undiluted by multiple perspectives and various interpretations. Solo performance is not a replacement, but an alternative to the traditional way things are done.

So, get out there and add your idiosyncratic voice to the cultural landscape. Craft a show for yourself and travel it around. Present it to different audiences in different places. That's what it comes down to: have adventures, make good art, tell good stories, have an impact on audiences. Let your own personal voice ring out.

And when you have done this, move on to making your next solo show.

Resources

History:

Young, Jordan R. (2012) *Acting Solo: The Art and Craft of Solo Performance.* Past Times Publishing Co. [Kindle edition].

Warren, Dorothy. (1999) *The World of Ruth Draper: A Portrait of an Actress.* Southern Illinois University Press.

Writing and Structure:

Booker, Christopher. (2005) *The Seven Basic Plots: Why We Tell Stories.* Continuum International Pub Group.

DePaul, Greg. (2016) *Bring the Funny: The Essential Companion for the Comedy Screenwriter.* Routledge.

Freytag, Gustav. (1900) *Freytag's Technique of the Drama: An Exposition of Dramatic Composition and Art. An Authorized Translation from the 6th German ed.* Translated by Elias J. MacEwan. Chicago. Scott, Foresman and Company.

Memorizing and Rehearsing:

Mooney, Timothy. (2011) *Acting at the Speed of Life: Conquering Theatrical Style*. TMRT Press.

DIY Media Training:

Cabane, Olivia Fox. (2022) *The Charisma Myth: How Anyone Can Master the Art and Science of Personal Magnetism*. Efinito.

McGowan, Bill. (2014) *Pitch Perfect: How to Say It Right the First Time, Every Time*. Harper Business.

Marketing:

Labrecque, Tammi L. (2018) *Newsletter Ninja: How to Become an Author Mailing List Expert*. Larks and Katydids Press.

Liner, Elaine. (2017) *107 Publicity Boosters That Work: How to Master the Media Matrix at Edinburgh Fringe, Every Other Fringe and Back in Your Own Hometown*. KDP Direct Publishing. Kindle Edition.

Other Resources:

Dicks, Matthew. (2018). *Storyworthy: Engage, Teach, Persuade, and Change Your Life Through the Power of Storytelling.* New World Library.

McEntire, Brad. (2021) *Chop: A One-Person Play.* Dribble Funk Books. [Kindle edition].

McEntire, Brad. (2020). "Chop: A Romance on the Outer Edge". [show website] https://dribblefunk.wixsite.com/chop

Ruth Draper. (2005) *Ruth Draper and Her Company of Characters: Selected Monologues.* [Audio CD]. BMG Special Products.

Waller-Bridge, Phoebe. (2019) *Fleabag: The Special Edition.* Nick Hern Books

Zabel, Morton Dauwen. (1960) *The Art of Ruth Draper: Her Dramas and Characters.* Doubleday.

About The Author

Brad McEntire is a native Texan and works primarily as a playwright, director, solo performer and educator. His plays have been produced/developed on stages around the world over the last twenty years. In 2015, McEntire served as the first theatre-artist-in-residence at the Kathy George Indie Artist Residency in Ashford, Oregon. He was named a winner of the 2018 Texas Playwrights Festival for his full-length play *Que Será, Giant Monster*.

Several collections of his plays have been published through Dribble Funk Books and are available on Amazon.com. He is also the creator of the webcomic series *Donnie Rocket Toaster-Face* and *The Ongoing Saga of J. Herbin*. McEntire is also the author of two children's picture books, *The Secret Island* and *Petey Gale Goes Up and Beyond*.

He is a satellite member of The Playwright's Center in Minneapolis, part of the New Play Exchange online and has studied playwriting with Will Power as part of the Dallas Playwrights Workshop at Southern Methodist University.

As a stage actor McEntire has performed throughout the United States. Additionally, he was a commercial actor with the Mary Collins Agency in Dallas, Texas from 2008-2015. For more than a decade McEntire has toured his original one-person shows *Chop*, *Cyrano A-Go-Go*, *Robert's Eternal Goldfish* and *The Beast of Hyperborea* to venues and festivals all over North America. He is also currently the Artistic Director of the small-batch theatre company Audacity Theatre Lab.

McEntire served as the founding producer of the Dallas Solo Fest (2014-2019) and between 2010-2020 served as chief editor of the website TheSoloPerformer.com [http://thesoloperformer.blogspot.com]. He produces and hosts a podcast called *The Cultivated Playwright*, where he talks about artistic issues and personal growth.

He has taught theatre to students of all ages, from elementary school kids to senior citizens. As an arts educator he was the head of a public high school theatre department for several years and has taught at the college level since 2002. He holds a B.F.A. in theatre and performance arts from the College of Santa Fe and a M.A. in theatre (with a concentration on playwriting) from Texas Woman's University.

McEntire lives outside of Dallas, Texas with his wife and son. Besides theatre activities, he enjoys camping, good cigars, reading, watching movies and travel. He is an outspoken advocate for indie theatre and, in particular, solo performance. He loves connecting with other artists as well as readers/ audience.

More information at: www.BradMcEntire.com and www.BradMcEntirePlays.com

Other Books by the Author

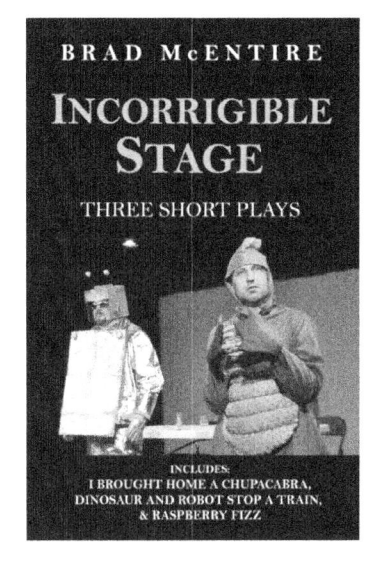

Available on Amazon.com